INSIGHTS INTO EDUCATION

Bringing about a totally new mind

J. Krishnamurti

Krishnamurti Foundation of America
Ojai, California

For additional information write to:

Krishnamurti Foundation of America
PO Box 1560
Ojai, CA 93024, United States

or

Krishnamurti Foundation Trust
Brockwood Park, Bramdean, Hampshire SO24 0LQ
United Kingdom

FIRST EDITION
Printed in the United States of America
Published by Krishnamurti Foundation of America

Editor: Stephen Smith
Associate editor: Alok Mathur

ISBN: 1539500446

Krishnamurti Foundation of America
www.kfa.org
www.jkrishnamurti.org
ISBN 13: 9781539500445

Also by J. Krishnamurti

Is it not the function of education to help man to bring about a total revolution? Most of us are concerned with partial revolution, economic or social. But the revolution of which I am talking is a total revolution of man at all the levels of his consciousness, of his life, of his being. That requires a great deal of understanding. It is not the result of any theory or any system of thought; on the contrary, no system of thought can produce a revolution: it can only produce a particular effect which is not a revolution. The revolution which is essential at the present time can only come into being when there is a total apprehension of the process in which man's mind works—not according to any particular religion or any particular philosophy or any system—the understanding of ourselves as a total process. That is the only revolution that can bring about lasting peace.

– J. Krishnamurti

TABLE OF CONTENTS

FOREWORD

Insights into Education presents the educational philosophy of J. Krishnamurti in an easy to use, topic-based format. It is a practical handbook, not a book for private study; indeed, as experience has shown, it comes alive best when used as an introduction to group investigation and dialogue. What it offers to teachers everywhere is an inroad into the many matters of concern with which they are faced on a daily basis. That we cannot continue as we have been doing, with rote-learning, fact-finding, and a modicum of analysis as the building blocks of education, is obvious to anyone who is at all aware—aware, that is, not only of the outer world with its amazing and accelerating technological advancement, but of the alienation, poverty, and despair, the "gutters and suicides" of our times. It is these very issues that are tackled here, sometimes implicitly but always at depth.

What Krishnamurti proposes, and here discloses, is a different approach to learning altogether, one that distinguishes itself radically from what we normally understand by that term: the accumulation of knowledge, with its application and testing. For, by thus narrowing down our understanding to the pragmatic and the measurable—a tendency, moreover, that is on the increase—we forfeit the opportunity to probe deeply and to awaken intelligence in our students and in ourselves. What is meant by *intelligence* in this context is not the capacity to memorize and measure, but that subtler ability to see the whole which comes alive in a human being when he/she sees the limits of the measurable. To awaken this intelligence is the goal of education.

> 'Intelligence is the capacity to perceive the es-
> sential, the *what is;* and to awaken this capacity,
> in oneself and in others, is education.'

> – J. Krishnamurti

Of course, the intelligence of which he speaks, which is really a shift in the dimension of learning, cannot be come upon solely by discussion. It requires the kind of orientation towards learning which sites it equally in the inner and the outer: as I learn about the world I am learning about myself. For, in terms of consciousness, the two are one.

But while challenging the basis and the thrust of education there are topics here that any teacher will recognize: *Freedom, Freedom and Order in School, Fear and Authority in School,* etc. Nor are these presented as the "final word"; on the contrary, each topic is intended for investigation, to be exposed and explored in actual situations. What is proposed is in no way dogmatic or canonical but rather that, in the spirit of inquiry, we open up the storehouse of the teachings so that their dynamic resonance can be felt and applied. In the context, for instance, of a dimensional shift it would be interesting to see in practical terms how this can be worked out in contemporary classrooms, including the approach to specific subjects.

There is no prescribed method as such; what there is are clear, overarching statements and a host of indicators as to how to proceed. Try *Listening, Looking, Learning* for starters.

Some of the topics were originally intended for the use of teachers talking with each other as part of a reflective meta-dialogue, and these are of a more philosophical nature. But in reviewing the material for publication now, the editor feels that there is little time, existentially or practically, for these once well-established, nice distinctions. The situation is too urgent; as Krishnamurti puts it, 'The house is burning.' We may even be doing the students a favour by opening up for them, easily and early, such abiding topics as fear, loneliness and death. For, surely, they are already aware of them and may even bring fresh insights to them. To many of us it is increasingly obvious that we are all in the same boat and that differences of age, sex, colour and class play very little part in the furtherance of true learning.

Stephen Smith: Ojai, California, May 2015

THE PURPOSE OF LIFE

Does life have a meaning, a purpose? Is not living in itself its own purpose, its own meaning? Why do we want more? Because we are so dissatisfied with our life; our life is so empty, so tawdry, so monotonous, doing the same thing over and over again, we want something more, something beyond that which we are doing. Since our everyday life is so empty, so dull, so meaningless, so boring, so intolerably stupid, we say life must have a fuller meaning . . .

A man who is living richly, a man who sees things as they are and is content with what he has, is not confused, he is clear; therefore he does not ask what is the purpose of life. For him, the very living is the beginning and the end. Our difficulty is that, since our life is empty, we want to find a purpose to life and strive for it. Such a purpose can only be mere intellection, without any reality; when the purpose of life is pursued by a stupid, dull mind, by an empty heart, that purpose will also be empty. Therefore our purpose is how to make our life rich, not with money and all the rest of it, but inwardly rich, which is not something cryptic. When you say that the purpose of life is to be happy, the purpose of life is to find God, that desire to find God is an escape from life and your

God is merely a thing that is known. You can only make your way towards an object which you know; if you build a staircase to the thing that you call God, surely that is not God.

Reality can be understood only in living, not in escape. When you seek a purpose of life you are really escaping and not understanding what life is. Life is relationship, life is action in relationship; when I do not understand relationship, or when relationship is confused, then I seek a fuller meaning. Why are our lives so empty? Why are we so lonely, frustrated? Because we have never looked into ourselves and understood ourselves. We never admit to ourselves that this life is all we know and that it should therefore be understood fully and completely. We prefer to run away from ourselves, and that is why we seek the purpose of life away from relationship.

If we begin to understand action, which is our relationship with people, with property, with beliefs and ideas, then we will find that relationship itself brings its own reward—you do not have to seek. It is like seeking love. Can you find love by seeking it? Love cannot be cultivated. You will find love only in relationship, not outside relationship, and it is because we have no love that we want a purpose of life. When there is love, which is its own eternity, then there is no search for God because love *is* God.

The First and Last Freedom, pp. 280-81

The questioner . . . explains in his letter that he is a married man, the father of several children, and is most anxious to be informed of the purpose of life. See the tragedy of it and do not laugh. You are all in the same position, are you not? You beget children, you are in responsible positions, and yet you are immature in thought, in life; you do not know love. How shall you find out the purpose of life? Shall another tell you? Must you not discover it for yourself? Is the purpose of life the routine of office work, year after year? Is it the pursuit of money, of position and power? Is it the achievement of an ambition? Is it the performance of rituals, those vain repetitions? Is it the acquisition of virtue, to be walled in by barren righteousness? None of these is the end purpose of life. Then what is? To find it, must you not go beyond all these? Only then will you find it.

The man of sorrow is not seeking the purpose of life, he wants to be free from sorrow. But, you see, you are not aware that you suffer. You suffer but escape from it, and so do not understand it. This question should reveal to you the ways of your mind and heart; the question is a self-revelation. You are in conflict, in confusion, in misery, which is the result of your own daily activities of thought and feeling. To understand this conflict, confusion and misery, you have to understand yourself, and as you understand, thought proceeds deeper and deeper until the end purpose is revealed. But to merely stand on the edge of confusion and ask the meaning of life has no meaning. A man who has lost the song of his heart, he is ever seeking, he is enchanted by the voice of others. He will find it again only when he ceases to follow, when his desire is still.

Madras 1947: Talk #8, CW Vol. IV, pp. 129-30

EDUCATION AND THE
PURPOSE OF LIFE

Questioner: What is right education? As teachers and as parents we are confused.

Krishnamurti: Now, how are we going to find the truth of this matter? Merely forcing the mind into a system, a pattern, is obviously not education. So, to discover what is right education, we must find out what we mean by education. Education is not to learn the purpose of life, but to understand the meaning, the significance, the process of existence; because if you say life has a purpose then the purpose is self-projected. To find out what is right education you have first to inquire into the whole significance of life, of living. What is present education? Learning to earn money, acquiring a trade, becoming an engineer, a sociologist, learning how to butcher people or how to read a poem. If you say education is to make a person efficient, which means to give him technical knowledge, then you must understand the whole significance of efficiency.

What happens when a person becomes more and more efficient? He becomes more and more ruthless. What are you doing in your daily life? What is happening now in the world?

Education means the development of a particular technique, which is efficiency, which means industrialization, the capacity to work faster and produce more and more, all of which ultimately leads to war. You see this happening every day. Education as it is leads to war, and what is the point of education? To destroy or be destroyed. So, obviously, the present system of education is utterly futile; therefore what is important is to educate the educator. These are not clever statements to be listened to and laughed off. Because without educating the teacher, what can he teach the child except the exploiting principles on which he himself has been brought up?

Most of you have read many books. Where are you? You have money or can earn it, you have your pleasures and ceremonies—and you are in conflict. What is the point of education, of learning to earn money, when your whole existence leads to misery and war? So, right education must begin with the educator, the parent, the teacher; and the inquiry into right education means inquiry into life, into existence, does it not? What is the point of your being educated as a lawyer if you are only going to increase conflict and maintain litigation? But there is money in that, and you thrive on it. So, if you want to bring about right education, you must obviously understand the meaning, the significance, of existence. It is not only to earn money, to have leisure, but to be able to think directly, truly—not *consistently,* because to think consistently is merely to conform to a pattern. A consistent thinker is a thoughtless person: he merely repeats certain phrases and thinks in a groove. To find out what is right education, there must be the understanding of existence, which means the understanding of yourself, because you cannot understand existence abstractly; you cannot understand yourself by theorizing as to what education should be. Right education begins with the right understanding of the educator.

Look at what is happening in the world: governments are taking control of education—naturally, because all governments are preparing for war. Your pet government, as well as the foreign government, must inevitably prepare for war. A sovereign government must have an army, a navy, an air force. To make the citizens efficient for war, to prepare them to perform their duties thoroughly, efficiently, ruthlessly, the central government must control them; therefore they educate them, as they manufacture mechanical instruments, to be ruthlessly efficient. If that is the purpose and end of education, to destroy or be destroyed, then it must be ruthless; and I am not at all sure that that is not what you want, because you are still educating your children in the same old fashion. Right education begins with the understanding of the educator, the teacher, which means that he must be free of established patterns of thought. Education is not merely imparting information, knowing how to read, gathering and correlating facts, but it is seeing the whole significance of education, of government, of the world situation, of the totalitarian spirit which is becoming more and more dominant throughout the world. Being confused, you create the educator who is also confused, and through so-called education you give power to destroy the foreign government. Therefore before you ask what right education is, you must understand yourself; and you will see that it does not take a long time to understand yourself if you are interested to find out. Without understanding yourself as the educator, how can you bring about a new kind of education? Therefore we come back to the eternal point, which is yourself. And you want to avoid that point, you want to shift the responsibility onto the teacher, onto the government. The government is what you are, the world is what you are; and without understanding yourself, how can there be right education?

Rajahmundry 1949: Talk #3, CW Vol. VI, pp. 20-22

THE AIMS OF EDUCATION

The ignorant man is not the unlearned but he who does not know himself, and the learned man is stupid when he relies on books, on knowledge and on authority to give him understanding. Understanding comes only through self-knowledge, which is awareness of one's total psychological process. Thus education, in the true sense, is the understanding of oneself, for it is within each one of us that the whole of existence is gathered. . . .

Without understanding ourselves, mere occupation leads to frustration, with its inevitable escapes through all kinds of mischievous activities. Technique without understanding leads to enmity and ruthlessness, which we cover up with pleasant-sounding phrases. Of what value is it to emphasize technique and become efficient entities if the result is mutual destruction? Our technical progress is fantastic, but it has only increased our powers of destroying one another, and there is starvation and misery in every land. . . .

The right kind of education, while encouraging the learning of a technique, should accomplish something which is of far greater importance; it should help man to experience the integrated process of life. It is this experiencing that will put capacity and technique in their right place. . . .

Ideals and blueprints for a perfect utopia will never bring about the radical change of heart which is essential if there is to be an end to war and universal destruction. Ideals cannot change our present values: they can be changed only by the right kind of education, which is to foster the understanding of *what is* . . .

The right kind of education is not concerned with any ideology, however much it may promise a future utopia: it is not based on any system, however carefully thought out; nor is it a means of conditioning the individual in some special manner. Education in the true sense is helping the individual to be mature and free, to flower greatly in love and goodness. . . .

Another function of education is to create new values. Merely to implant existing values in the mind of the child, to make him conform to ideals, is to condition him without awakening his intelligence. Education is intimately related to the present world crisis, and the educator who sees the causes of this universal chaos should ask himself how to awaken intelligence in the student, thus helping the coming generation not to bring about further conflict and disaster. He must give all his thought, all his care and affection to the creation of the right environment and to the development of understanding, so that when the child grows into maturity he will be capable of dealing intelligently with the human problems that confront him. But in order to do this, the educator must understand himself instead of relying on ideologies, systems and beliefs.

Education and the Significance of Life, pp. 17-25

To really tackle the problem of what is true education, to understand the whole significance of education, why we are educated, what it is all about, is an immense thing not just to be talked about for a few minutes. You may have read or be capable of reading many books, you may have great knowledge, an infinite variety of explanations, but that is not freedom. Freedom comes with the understanding of oneself, and it is only such freedom that can meet without fear every crisis, every influence that conditions; but that requires a great deal of penetration, meditation.

New York 1954: Talk #3, CW Vol. VIII, p. 227

EDUCATING THE EDUCATOR

Questioner: May we know your ideas on education and how it can be imparted?

Krishnamurti: This is an enormous subject, and to try to answer it in a few minutes is quite absurd because its implications are so vast, but we will state it as clearly and as simply as possible because there is a great joy in seeing a thing clearly without being influenced by other people's notions and ideas and instructions, whether they be the government or the specialists or the very learned in education. What has happened in the world after centuries of education? We have had two catastrophic wars which have almost destroyed man, that is, man as a means of knowledge. We see that education has failed because it has resulted in the most dreadful destruction that the world has ever known. So, what has happened? Seeing that education has failed, governments are stepping in to control education. They want to control the way in which you should be educated, what you think—not how you think, but what you think. So, when the government steps in there is regimentation, as has happened throughout the world. Governments are not concerned with the happiness of the masses, but they are concerned with producing an efficient machine; and as our age is a technical age, they want technicians who will create the marvellous modern machine called society. These technicians will function efficiently and therefore automatically. This is what is happening in the world, whether the government is of the left or of the right. They do not want you to think, but if you do think then you must think along a particular line or according to what religious organizations say. We have been through this process, the control by the organized religion, by the priests and by the government. It has resulted in disaster and in the exploitation of man. Whether man is exploited in the name of God or in the name of the government, it is the same thing. As man is human he eventually breaks up the system. So, that is one of the problems. As long as education is the handmaiden of the government there is no hope. This is the tendency we find everywhere in the world at the present time, whether it is inspired by the right or by the left, because if you are left free to think for yourself you may revolt and therefore you will have to be liquidated. There are various methods of liquidation which we need not go into.

In considering education we will have to find out the purpose of education, the purpose of living. If that is not clear to you, why educate yourself? What is significant? What are we living for? What are we struggling for? If that is not clear to you, education has no significance, has it? One period will be technical, another period will be religious, the next period will be something else again and so on. We are talking about a system and so is it not important to find out what it is all about? Are you merely being educated in order to get a job? Then you make living a means to a job and you make of yourself a man to fit into a groove. Is that the purpose? We must think of this problem in that light and not merely repeat slogans. To a life that is not free from systems, whether they be

modern or ancient, free of even the most advanced and pro-
gressive ideas, education will have no meaning. If you do not
know why you are living, what the purpose of being educated
is, then why make so much fuss about how you are educated?
As it is, you are . . . becoming cannon fodder. If that is what
we want, then certainly we must make ourselves extremely efficient to kill each other; and that is what is happening, is it
not? There are more armies, more armaments, more money
invested in producing bacteriological warfare and atomic destruction than ever before, and in order to accomplish all this
you must be technicians of the highest order, and therefore
you are becoming tools of destruction. Is not all this due to
education? You are becoming fodder for cannons, regiment-
ed minds. Or else you become an industrialist, a businessman
grabbing after money, and if this does not interest you, you
become addicted to knowledge, to books, or you aspire to be
a scientist caught in his laboratory. If there is any higher purpose to our lives and we do not discover it, then life has very
little significance; it is as if we committed suicide. And we *are*
committing suicide when we make ourselves into machines,
either religious machines or political machines. So if we do
not discover what the purpose of life is, education has very
little significance.

Then what is the need or the purpose of our living? I am
not telling you, and do not expect me to tell you: we are taking the journey together. We must turn our back against divisions and distinctions, that is, we must find what is the real,
what is God, what is eternity and what is happiness. A man
who is already happy is not bothered at all. A man in love
loves everybody. For him there is no class distinction; he does
not want to liquidate somebody because that somebody has
more. If happiness is the end then what we are doing now

has no significance. To find reality there must be freedom, freedom from conditioned thinking, so as to discover if there is not something beyond the sensate values—not the absurd political freedom but freedom from conditioning, from the psychological demands that condition thought. Does freedom come through education, through any system of government, whether of the left or of the right? Can parents, environment give freedom? If so, environment becomes extraordinarily important because parents must be educated as well as the educator. If the educator is confused, conditioned, narrow, limited, bound by superstitious ideas, whether modern or ancient, the child will suffer. The educator therefore is far more important, that is, to educate the educator is far more important than educating the child. That means the parents and the teachers should be educated first. Do they want to be educated, altered or revolutionized? Not in the least, for the very simple reason that they want permanency. They want status quo, things as they are, with wars and competition and a political world in which everybody is confused, pulling at each other, destroying each other.

You ask me what I should do about education. It is too vast a subject. If you want things to be continued as they are then you must accept the present system which brings constant wars and confusion, never a moment of peace in the world. It is much more difficult to educate the educator than the child because the educator has already grown stupid. I do not think you realize what is happening in the world, how catastrophic it all is. The educator is becoming dull, and he does not know what to do. He is confused; he goes from one system to another, from one teacher to another, from the latest to the most ancient, and yet he does not find what he is looking for,

for the very simple reason that he has not located the source of confusion, which is himself. How can such a man awaken intelligence in another? So, that is one of the problems.

What is the child? He is a product of yourself, is he not? So he is already conditioned. He is the result of the past and the present. The idea that if given freedom the child would develop naturally seems to be fallacious because, after all, the child is the father and the father is the child, though with certain modifications of tendencies. To give freedom to a child, you must first understand yourself, the giver of freedom, the educator. If I have to educate a child but do not understand myself and so start with my conditioned response, how can I teach him? How can I awaken intelligence in him? So, that is part of the problem. Then there is the question of nourishment, care and love. Most of us have no real love for our children though we talk about it. Education is something tremendous, and without love I do not possibly see how there can be education. The moment you love somebody, you understand the person, your heart is in it. Do we love our children? Do we love our wives or husbands? Do we love our neighbours? We do not, because if we did there would be a different world. There is no true education through a system. If we love there must be instantaneous communication, on the same level and at the same time, and because we ourselves are dry, empty, governments and systems have taken over.

I am afraid you will say that I have said nothing positive about education. Is not negative thinking the highest form of thinking? For wisdom comes through negation. Do not put what I say into your old bottles and thus lose the perfume. To transform the world there must be regeneration within ourselves. We find we have blueprints to educate our children but, naturally, blueprints have no love; therefore you produce machines. We have brains, but what has happened to them? We are becoming cannon fodder. We are not creators, we are not thinkers. We do not know how to love; we are merely drudging with our routine minds and naturally we become inefficient. And the government which wants efficiency for destruction is going to make us efficient. There is an efficiency inspired by love which is greater than the efficiency of machinery.

Madras 1947: Talk #5, CW Vol. IV, pp. 106-08

THE INDIVIDUAL AND SOCIETY

Questioner: The modern educational system is a failure, as it has produced two devastating wars and appalling misery. Learning to read and write and acquiring various techniques, which is the cultivation of memory, is obviously not enough, for it has produced unspeakable sorrow. What do you consider to be the end purpose of education?

Krishnamurti: Is it not to bring about an integrated individual? If that is the purpose of education, then we must be clear as to whether the individual exists for society or whether society exists for the individual. If society needs and uses the individual for its own purposes, then it is not concerned with the cultivation of an integrated human being; what it wants is an efficient machine, a conforming and respectable citizen, and this requires only a very superficial integration. As long as the individual obeys and is willing to be thoroughly conditioned, society will find him useful and will spend time and money on him. But if society exists for the individual, then it must help in freeing him from its own conditioning influence. It must educate him to be an integrated human being.

Commentaries on Living II, pp. 46-47

Is it not important to ask ourselves, each one of us, whether we are really individuals and not merely assert that we are? Actually, we are not. You may have a separate body, a different face, a different name and family, but the inward structure of your mind is essentially conditioned by society; therefore you are not an individual. Only the mind that is not bound by the impositions of society, with all the implications involved, can be free to find out that which is true and that which is God. Otherwise, all we do is merely to repeat catastrophe; otherwise, there is no possibility of that revolution which will bring about a totally different kind of world. It seems to me that is the only important thing—not to what society, to what group, to what religion you should or should not belong, which has all become so infantile, immature, but for you to find out for yourself if the mind can be totally free from all the impositions of custom, tradition and belief, and thereby be free to find out what is true. Then only can we be creative human beings.

Amsterdam 1955: Talk #2, CW Vol. IX, p. 9

FEAR, ANXIETY, EMPTINESS

We are asking why there is this sense of want, why there is not a sense of complete self-sufficiency. Why is there this longing for something in order to fulfil or to cover up something? Is it because for most of us there is a sense of emptiness, loneliness, a sense of void? Physiologically we need food, clothes and shelter—that one must have—but that is denied when there is political, religious, economic division, nationalistic division, which is the curse of this world, which has been invented by the Western world; it did not exist in the Eastern world, this spirit of nationality; it has come recently into being there too, this poison. When there is division between peoples, between nationalities and between beliefs, dogmas, security for everybody becomes almost impossible. The tyrannical world of dictatorship is trying to provide that, food for everybody, but it cannot achieve it. We all know that, we can move from that.

So, what is it that we lack? Knowledge? Knowledge being the accumulation of experience, psychological, scientific and in other directions, which is knowledge in the past. Knowledge *is* the past. Is this what we want? Is this what we miss? Is this what we are educated for, to gather all the knowledge we can possibly have, to act skilfully in the technological world? Or is there a sense of lack, want, psychologically, inwardly? Which means you will try to fill that inward emptiness, that lack, through or with experience, which is the accumulated knowledge. So you are trying to fill that emptiness, that void, that sense of immense loneliness, with something which thought has created. Therefore desire arises from this urge to fill that emptiness. After all, when you are seeking enlightenment, or self-realization as the Hindus call it, it is a form of desire. This sense of ignorance will be wiped away or put aside or dissipated by acquiring tremendous knowledge, enlightenment. It is never the process of investigating *what is* but rather of acquiring, not actually looking at *what is* but inviting something which might be, or hopeful of a greater experience, greater knowledge. So we are always avoiding *what is*. The *what is* is created by thought. My loneliness, emptiness, sorrow, pain, suffering, anxiety, fear—that is actually *what is*. And thought is incapable of facing it and tries to move away from it.

Truth and Actuality, pp. 75-76

EMPTINESS, LONELINESS,
SORROW, DEATH

This is not some abstract theory; it is your own life as you actually live it from day to day. I am describing it, but don't be satisfied with the description; be aware of yourself through the description and you will see how your life is caught up in the various means of escape. That is why it is so important to look at the fact, to consider, to explore, to go deeply into *what is*, because *what is* has no time, no future. *What is* is eternal; *what is* is life; *what is* is death; *what is* is love, in which there is no fulfilment or frustration. These are the facts, the actual realities of existence, but a mind that has been nurtured and conditioned in the various avenues of escape finds it extraordinarily difficult to look at *what is*; therefore it devotes years to the study of symbols and myths about which volumes have been written, or it loses itself in ceremonies or in the practise of a method, a system, a discipline.

What is important, surely, is to observe the fact and not cling to opinions or merely discuss the symbol which represents the fact. . . . The symbol is the word. Take death. The word *death* is the symbol used to convey all the implications of the fact—fear, sorrow, the extraordinary sense of loneliness, of emptiness, of littleness and isolation, of deep, abiding frustration. With the word *death* we are all familiar, but very few of us ever see the implications of that fact. We almost never look into the face of death and understand the extraordinary things that are implied in it. We prefer to escape through the belief in a world hereafter, or we cling to theory of reincarnation. We have these comforting explanations, a veritable multitude of ideas, of assertions and denials, with all the symbols and myths that go with them. . . . This is a fact.

Bombay 1960: Talk #6, CW Vol. XI, p. 286

BEING ALONE WITH DEATH

To come upon the truth, every form of identification must end, every form of fear, every desire for comfort. One must not be caught in that illusion which says there is a marvellous state after death. The mind must have no identification with the name, with the form, or with any person, idea, conclusion. Is that possible? That does not deny love; on the contrary, when one is attached to a person there is no love, there is dependence, there is the fear of being left alone in the world where everything is so insecure, both psychologically and outwardly. To find out what is the truth of death, what is the meaning, the real depth of that extraordinary thing that must happen, there must be freedom. And there is no freedom when there is attachment, when there is fear, when there is a desire for comfort. Can one put all that aside? To find the truth of this extraordinary thing called death one must also find the truth of what is before death; not the truth after death but also the truth before death. What is the truth before death? If that is not clear the other cannot be clear. One must look very closely, carefully and freely at what is before death, which we call living. What is the truth of one's living? Which means what is one, or who is one, which one calls living? A heavily conditioned mind brought about through education, environment, culture, through religious sanctions, beliefs and dogmas, rituals, *my country, your country*; the constant battle, wanting to be happy and being unhappy, depressed and elated, going through anxiety, uncertainty, hate, envy, fear and the pursuit of pleasure; afraid to be alone, fear of loneliness, old age, disease—this is the truth of our life, our daily life. Can such a mind which has not put order in this life—order in the sense of that which comes through clarity and compassion—can such a mind which is so utterly fragmented, disorderly, frightened, find out the truth about something outside of all that?

The Wholeness of Life, pp. 210-11

THE CONDITIONING PROCESS

If the totality of my thinking process is the response of my conditioning—which it is—the mind can never discover what is true and whether there is anything which has not already been experienced. If the mind is to discover something totally new, it must come to this point when it is in a state of not-knowing. That is why it is very important to go into this whole problem of consciousness—consciousness being the totality of all experience, of all memory, the residue of the past. One must know oneself, for self-knowledge is essential if one is to find out whether the mind can ever be free of all knowledge and discover something new.

If we look into ourselves we shall see that experience conditions the mind. Every new experience is translated in terms of the old; it is absorbed by the established pattern of mediocrity and tradition. A mind that is caught in tradition, in mediocrity, can never find out what is true; it can never discover that which is unimaginable, which cannot be conceived of, described or believed in.

So, can the mind free itself from tradition and conformity—not only from those imposed by environment but from the tradition and conformity which are built up by the mind itself through experience? One can see very well that all one's thinking is the response of one's conditioning. Our reaction to a challenge is always according to the background in which we have been brought up, and so long as we do not know our own conditioning, our thinking is never free. We may be able to adjust ourselves to a new pattern, a new way of life, to new beliefs, to new dogmas, but in that process thought never frees itself.

So, one has to inquire very deeply within oneself as to the significance and purpose of memory. Is memory the totality of our consciousness? Consciousness is within the field of time, is it not? My thinking, which is the result of the past, colours the present and projects the future—and this is the process of time. So all my experience is within the field of time. Can the mind free itself from that whole process? And if it does free itself, can it discover something new? . . .

The mind responds to any challenge through its previously accumulated knowledge. Either its response is adequate or inadequate. When it responds adequately there is no conflict, no suffering; but when there is inadequacy of response then there is suffering, there is conflict. This is obvious and superficial. To know ourselves we must inquire much more profoundly; we must understand the whole process of our consciousness, the totality of it, not merely the superficial consciousness of daily activities but the deep unconscious which contains the whole residue of racial conditioning, the racial memories, the hidden motives, urges, compulsions, fixations. This does not mean that we must go to a psychologist; on the contrary, we must understand ourselves through direct experience.

To have this self-knowledge, the mind must be aware of itself from moment to moment; it must see all its own movements—its urges, its motives, the operations of memory—and how, through tradition, it is caught in mediocrity. If the mind can be aware of all that within itself, then you will find there is a possibility of being free from all conditioning and discovering something totally new. Then the mind itself is made new. And perhaps that is the real, the immeasurable.

Brussels 1956: Talk #4, CW Vol. X, pp. 50-51

The problem is that most of us reject one particular form of conditioning and find another form—a wider, more significant, or more pleasant conditioning. . . . Such substitution is obviously not understanding life, life being relationship. Our problem is how to be free from *all* conditioning. Either you say it is impossible—that no human mind can ever be free from conditioning—or you begin to experiment, to inquire, to discover. If you assert that it is impossible, obviously you are out of the running. Your assertion may be based on limited or wide experience, or on the mere acceptance of a belief; but such assertion is the denial of search, of research, of inquiry, of discovery. To find out if it is possible for the mind to be completely free from all conditioning, you must be free to inquire and to discover. . . .

The understanding of the whole process of conditioning does not come to you through analysis or introspection, because the moment you have the analyzer, that very analyzer himself is part of the background, and therefore his analysis is of no significance. . . . The analyzer who examines, who analyzes the thing which he is looking at is himself part of the conditioned state, and therefore whatever his interpretation, his understanding, his analysis may be, it is still part of the background. So that way there is no escape. . . . To analyze the past, to arrive at conclusions through a series of experimentations, to make assertions and denials and all the rest of it, implies in its very essence the continuance of the background in different forms. When you see the truth of that fact then you will discover that the analyzer has come to an end. . . . Then there is no entity apart from the background; there is only thought as the background, thought being the response of memory, both conscious and unconscious, individual and collective.

So, the mind is the result of the past, which is the process of conditioning, and how is it possible for the mind to be free? To be free, the mind must not only see and understand its pendulum-like swing between the past and the future, but also be aware of the interval between thoughts. That interval is spontaneous; it is not brought about through any causation, through any wish, through any compulsion. . . .

You *are* the background, you are not separate; there is no thinker apart from the background, and the response of that background is what you call thinking. That background, whether it is cultured or uncultured, learned or ignorant, is constantly responding to any challenge, to any stimulant— and that response creates not only the so-called present but also the future—and that is our process of thinking.

If you watch very carefully you will see that though the response, the movement of thought, seems so swift there are gaps, there are intervals between thoughts. Between two thoughts there is a period of silence which is not related to the thought process. If you observe you will see that that period of silence, that interval, is not of time; and the discovery of that interval, the full experiencing of that interval, liberates you from conditioning—or rather, it does not liberate "you", but there is liberation from conditioning.

Bombay 1950: Talk #3, CW Vol. VI, pp. 109-10

EDUCATION AND THE
CONDITIONING PROCESS

The child is the result of both the past and the present and is therefore already conditioned. If we transmit our background to the child, we perpetuate both his and our own conditioning. There is radical transformation only when we understand our own conditioning and are free of it. . . .

While the children are young, we must of course protect them from physical harm and prevent them from feeling physically insecure. But unfortunately we do not stop there; we want to shape their ways of thinking and feeling, we want to mould them in accordance with our own cravings and intentions. We seek to fulfil ourselves in our children, to perpetuate ourselves through them. We build walls around them, condition them by our beliefs and ideologies, fears and hopes—and then we cry and pray when they are killed or maimed in wars, or otherwise made to suffer by the experiences of life.

Such experiences do not bring about freedom; on the contrary, they strengthen the will of the self. The self is made up of a series of defensive and expansive reactions, and its fulfilment is always in its own projections and gratifying identifications. As long as we translate experience in terms of the self, of the "me" and the "mine", as long as the "I", the ego, maintains itself through its reactions, experience cannot be freed from conflict, confusion and pain. Freedom comes only when one understands the ways of the self, the experiencer. It is only when the self, with its accumulated reactions, is not the experiencer that experience takes on an entirely different significance and becomes creation.

If we would help the child to be free from the ways of the self, which cause so much suffering, then each one of us should set about altering deeply his attitude and relationship to the child. Parents and educators, by their own thought and conduct, can help the child to be free and to flower in love and goodness.

Education as it is at present in no way encourages the understanding of the inherited tendencies and environmental influences which condition the mind and heart and sustain fear, and therefore it does not help us to break through these conditionings and bring about an integrated human being. Any form of education that concerns itself with a part and not with the whole of man inevitably leads to increasing conflict and suffering.

It is only in individual freedom that love and goodness can flower; and the right kind of education alone can offer this freedom. Neither conformity to the present society nor the promise of a future utopia can ever give to the individual that insight without which he is constantly creating problems. . . . Surely it is possible to help the individual to perceive the enduring values of life, without conditioning.

Education and the Significance of Life, pp. 27-29

RELATIONSHIP OF THE TEACHER WITH THE STUDENT

One has to find out what is the relationship of the teacher to the student. . . . Is he merely an informer, giving information to the child? Any machine can do that. . . . What is his relationship? Does he put himself on a pedestal, up there, and his student down there? Or is the relationship between the teacher and the student . . . a relationship in which there is learning on the part of the teacher as well as the student? Learning. Not I have learned and I am going to teach you—in that there is a division between the teacher and the student. But when there is learning on the part of the teacher as well as on the part of the student, there is no division: both are learning.

A Wholly Different Way of Living, pp. 62-63

Krishnamurti: I would like to . . . ask, what is the relationship between the educator and the person to be educated . . . what is the relationship between the two, not theoretically but actually? What is your relationship, as a teacher, to the student . . . when you and he realize that you are both conditioned?

What is the quality of relationship? And then we can discuss whether time is necessary, a longer time or a shorter time. I think that is an important thing to find out. . . . I want to find out what is the relationship between you and me when we realize that we are conditioned.

Questioner: I am not sure I quite understand the question, what is the relationship?

K: Before, our relationship was a teacher talking down to the student, informing him—not about himself but about the subject which he is teaching. But here we are asking, apart from that—because we are concerned with the total development of a human being—what is the relationship when two people realize that they are conditioned? Realize, not verbally but actually. This conditioning keeps people apart.

Q: If I am conditioned as the teacher then I can't actually help.

K: Not as a teacher but as a human being you are conditioned, and so is the other human being. What is the relationship between you two?

Q: We are both the same, surely.

K: Yes, but I said, when you realize.

Q: From that point onwards you can begin to work together.

Brockwood 1979
Conversation with Teachers #3, 23rd June

THE CHILD AND THE ADULT

Most children are curious, they want to know; but their eager inquiry is dulled by our pontifical assertions, our superior impatience, and our casual brushing aside of their curiosity. We do not encourage their inquiry, for we are rather apprehensive of what may be asked of us; we do not foster their discontent, for we ourselves have ceased to question.

Most parents and teachers are afraid of discontent because it is disturbing to all forms of security, and so they encourage the young to overcome it through safe jobs, inheritance, marriage, and the consolation of religious dogmas. Elders, knowing only too well the many ways of blunting the mind and the heart, proceed to make the child as dull as they are by impressing upon him the authorities, traditions and beliefs which they themselves have accepted.

Only by encouraging the child to question the book, whatever it be, to inquire into the validity of the existing social values, traditions, forms of government, religious beliefs and so on, can the educator and the parents hope to awaken and sustain his critical alertness and keen insight.

The young, if they are at all alive, are full of hope and discontent; they must be, otherwise they are already old and dead. The old are those who were once discontented but who have successfully smothered that flame and have found security and comfort in various ways. They crave permanency for themselves and their families, they ardently desire certainty in ideas, in relationships, in possessions; so the moment they feel discontented, they become absorbed in their responsibilities, in their jobs, or in anything else, in order to escape from that disturbing feeling of discontent.

While we are young is the time to be discontented, not only with ourselves but also with the things about us. We should learn to think clearly and without bias, so as not to be inwardly dependent and fearful. Independence is not for that coloured section of the map which we call our country, but for ourselves as individuals; and though outwardly we are dependent on one another, this mutual dependence does not become cruel or oppressive if inwardly we are free of the craving for power, position and authority.

We must understand discontent, of which most of us are afraid. Discontent may bring what appears to be disorder; but if it leads, as it should, to self-knowledge and self-abnegation, then it will create a new social order and enduring peace. With self-abnegation comes immeasurable joy.

Discontent is the means to freedom; but in order to inquire without bias there must be none of the emotional dissipation which often takes the form of political gatherings, the shouting of slogans, the search for a guru or spiritual teacher, and religious orgies of different kinds. This dissipation dulls the mind and heart, making them incapable of insight and therefore easily moulded by circumstances and fear. It is the burning desire to inquire, and not the easy imitation of the multitude, that will bring about a new understanding of the ways of life.

The young are so easily persuaded by the priest or the politician, by the rich or the poor, to think in a particular way; but the right kind of education should help them to be watchful of these influences so that they do not repeat slogans like parrots or fall into any cunning trap of greed, whether their own or that of another. They must not allow authority to stifle their minds and hearts. To follow another, however great, or to give one's adherence to a gratifying ideology, will not bring about a peaceful world.

When we leave school or college, many of us put away books and seem to feel that we are done with learning; and there are those who are stimulated to think further afield, who keep on reading and absorbing what others have said, and become addicted to knowledge. As long as there is the worship of knowledge or technique as a means to success and dominance, there must be ruthless competition, antagonism, and the ceaseless struggle for bread.

As long as success is our goal we cannot be rid of fear, for the desire to succeed inevitably breeds the fear of failure. That is why the young should not be taught to worship success. Most people seek success in one form or another, whether on the tennis court, in the business world, or in politics. We all want to be on top, and this desire creates constant conflict within ourselves and with our neighbours; it leads to competition, envy, animosity, and finally to war.

Like the older generation, the young also seek success and security; though at first they may be discontented, they soon become respectable and are afraid to say no to society. The walls of their own desires begin to enclose them, and they fall in line and assume the reins of authority. Their discontent, which is the very flame of inquiry, of search, of understanding, grows dull and dies away, and in its place there comes the desire for a better job, a rich marriage, a successful career, all of which is the craving for more security.

There is no essential difference between the old and the young, for both are slaves to their own desires and gratifications. Maturity is not a matter of age, it comes with understanding. The ardent spirit of inquiry is perhaps easier for the young because those who are older have been battered about by life, conflicts have worn them out, and death in different forms awaits them. This does not mean that they are incapable of purposive inquiry but only that it is more difficult for them.

Many adults are immature and rather childish, and this is a contributing cause of the confusion and misery in the world. It is the older people who are responsible for the prevailing economic and moral crisis; and one of our unfortunate weaknesses is that we want someone else to act for us and change the course of our lives. We wait for others to revolt and build anew, and we remain inactive until we are assured of the outcome.

It is security and success that most of us are after; and a mind that is seeking security, that craves success, is not intelligent, and is therefore incapable of integrated action. There can be integrated action only if one is aware of one's own conditioning, of one's racial, national, political and religious prejudices, that is, only if one realizes that the ways of the self are ever separative.

Life is a well of deep waters. One can come to it with small buckets and draw only a little water, or one can come with large vessels, drawing plentiful waters that will nourish and sustain. While one is young is the time to investigate, to experiment with everything. A school should help its young people to discover their vocations and responsibilities, and not merely cram their minds with facts and technical knowledge;

it should be the soil in which they can grow without fear, happily and integrally.

To educate a child is to help him to understand freedom and integration. To have freedom there must be order, which virtue alone can give; and integration can take place only when there is great simplicity. From innumerable complexities we must grow to simplicity; we must become simple in our inward life and in our outward needs.

Education is at present concerned with outward efficiency, and it utterly disregards, or deliberately perverts, the inward nature of man; it develops only one part of him and leaves the rest to drag along as best it can. Our inner confusion, antagonism and fear ever overcome the outer structure of society, however nobly conceived and cunningly built. When there is not the right kind of education we destroy one another, and physical security for every individual is denied. To educate the student rightly is to help him to understand the total process of himself; for it is only when there is integration of the mind and heart in everyday action that there can be intelligence and inward transformation.

While offering information and technical training, education should above all encourage an integrated outlook on life; it should help the student to recognize and break down in himself all social distinctions and prejudices, and discourage the acquisitive pursuit of power and domination. It should encourage the right kind of self-observation and the experiencing of life as a whole, which is not to give significance to the part, to the "me" and the "mine", but to help the mind to go above and beyond itself to discover the real.

Education and the Significance of Life, pp. 41-46

THE OBSERVATION OF RELATIONSHIP

Can I observe myself through relationship? Can I know myself fundamentally, basically—all the reactions, all the nuances, the subtleties of myself—in relationship? So we have to inquire into what we mean by relationship—the word itself. To be related is to be in contact, to be not only physically intimate but to meet at the same level, at the same moment, with the same intensity. That is relationship. There is a relationship between a man and woman, or one friend and another, or a boy and girl, when they meet not merely physically, but much more. When they meet at the same level, at the same moment, with the same intensity, that can be called a real, true, actual relationship.

One's relationship with another is based on memory, on the various images, pictures, conclusions I have drawn about you and you have drawn about me, the various images that I have about you as wife, husband, girl or boy or friend, and so on. So, there is always image making. This is simple, this is normal; this is what actually goes on. When one is married to or lives with a girl or a boy, every incident, every word, every action creates an image. Are we clear on this point? Don't agree with me, please; I am not trying to persuade you to anything, but actually you can see it for yourself. A word is registered; if it is pleasant you purr, if it is unpleasant you immediately shrink from it, and that creates an image. The pleasure creates an image; the shrinking, the withdrawal creates an image. So, our actual relationship with each other is based on various subtle forms of pictures, images and conclusions. When that takes place, what happens?

On Learning and Knowledge, pp. 69-70

RELATIONSHIP WITH THE WORLD
AND PEOPLE

All your religions say, suppress the senses, suppress the reaction of the senses. We are saying quite the contrary, which means the awakening of the senses—not one particular sense—so that there is a total reaction of all the senses when you see a tree. When you look at the tree with all your senses there is no centre from which you are looking. When there is a centre, which is the ego, the "me", the self, the super-self, super-consciousness—it is still the self—when there is that self you cannot look at the beauty of a tree.

So, to bring about order naturally, without effort or the search for order, we must understand what is disorder, which is to understand our relationship not only to nature—the trees, the rivers, the birds, all the beautiful, extraordinary world in which we live—but also to understand the relationship between each other, man and woman. Do you understand your relationship with your wife or with your husband, or your relationship to the guru who is slightly neurotic? Have you ever looked at your relationship to your children? . . . If we don't understand relationship, that in itself brings about disorder, which is conflict between man and woman, or between each other. So, one must understand to have order in the house—not the external house but the house in which I live all the time, which is myself. If there is no order there, I will never have order with the universe, because the universe is living in total order: the sun rises, the sun sets, the seasons return—all the extraordinary things that are happening in the universe—without cause and therefore with order.

We live in disorder because we have causes. The cause is either reward or punishment. That is the basic cause in our life: I will do things if I am rewarded or if I am punished. When, because of the engine driver, the train arrives seven or ten hours late, that is disorder, it is utterly irresponsible. And nobody says anything to him. But if you frighten him or reward him, he becomes orderly. If the guru rewards the disciple or punishes him, it is the same thing. So, we depend on others to bring about order in our life; and that very dependence is disorder because we are then not responsible for what we are doing.

Rajghat, Varanasi 1981: Talk #1, 25ᵗʰ November

There must be order, something living and beautiful, not a mechanical thing: the order of the universe, the order that exists in mathematics, the order that exists in nature, in the relationship between various animals, an order that human beings have totally denied because in ourselves we are in disorder—which means that we are fragmentary, contradictory and frightened.

I am asking myself, and you are asking yourself, whether the mind is capable of learning, because it doesn't know what order is. It knows reaction to disorder, but the mind must discover whether it is actually capable of learning without reaction and can therefore be free to observe. In other words, is your mind aware of the problem of control, of discipline, of authority, and the constant response of reaction—are you aware of that whole structure? Are you aware of all this in yourself as you live from day to day? Or are you only aware when it is pointed out to you? Please see the difference. If you are aware of this whole problem of confusion, discipline, control and suppression, which is conformity, because you have been observing, living and watching, then it is your own; the other is second-hand. Now, which is it?

The Awakening of Intelligence, pp. 311-12

RELATIONSHIP TO NATURE
(WORKING WITH ONE'S HANDS)

Questioner: What is the meaning of right relationship with nature?

Krishnamurti: Sir, I do not know if you have discovered your relationship with nature. There is no "right relationship", there is only the understanding of relationship. "Right relationship" implies the mere acceptance of a formula, as does right thought. Right thought and right thinking are two different things. Right thought is merely conforming to what is right, what is respectable, whereas right thinking is movement, it is the product of understanding; and understanding is constantly undergoing modification, change. Similarly, there is a difference between right relationship and understanding our relationship with nature. What is your relationship with nature?—nature being the rivers, the trees, the swift-flying birds, the fish in the water, the minerals under the earth, the waterfalls and shallow pools. What is your relationship to them?

Most of us are not aware of that relationship. We never look at a tree, or if we do it is with a view of using that tree, either to sit in its shade or to cut it down for lumber. In other words, we look at trees with utilitarian purpose; we never look at a tree without projecting ourselves and utilizing it for our own convenience. We treat the earth and its products in the same way. There is no love of earth, there is only usage of earth. If one really loved the earth, there would be frugality in using the things of the earth. That is, if we were to understand our relationship with the earth, we should be very careful in the use we made of the things of the earth. The understanding of one's relationship with nature is as difficult as understanding one's relationship with one's neighbour, wife and children. But we have not given a thought to it, we have never sat down to look at the stars, the moon, or the trees. We are too busy with social or political activities. Obviously these activities are escapes from ourselves; and to worship nature is also an escape from ourselves.

We are always using nature, either as an escape or for utilitarian ends: we never actually stop and love the earth or the things of the earth. We never enjoy the rich fields, though we utilize them to feed and clothe ourselves. We never like to till the earth with our hands—we are ashamed to work with our hands. There is an extraordinary thing that takes place when you work the earth with your hands. But this work is done only by the lower castes; we upper classes are much too important, apparently, to use our own hands! So, we have lost our relationship with nature.

If once we understood that relationship, its real significance, then we would not divide property into yours and mine; though one might own a piece of land and build a house on it, it would not be "mine" or "yours" in the exclusive sense; it would be more a means of taking shelter. We do not love the earth and the things of the earth but merely utilize them, we are insensitive to the beauty of a waterfall, we have lost the touch of life, we have never sat with our backs against the trunk of a tree; and since we do not love nature, we do not know how to love human beings and animals. Go down the street and watch how the bullocks are treated, their tails all out of shape. You shake your head and say it's very sad. We have lost the sense of tenderness, that sensitivity, that response to things of beauty; and it is only in the renewal of that sensitivity that we can have understanding of what is true relationship. That sensitivity does not come in the mere hanging of a few pictures, or in painting a tree, or putting a few flowers in your hair: sensitivity comes only when this utilitarian outlook is put aside. It does not mean that you cannot use the earth, but you must use the earth as it is to be used. Earth is there to be loved, to be cared for, not to be divided as "yours" and "mine". It is foolish to plant a tree in a compound and call it "mine". It is only when one is free of exclusiveness that there is a possibility of having sensitivity, not only to nature but to human beings and to the ceaseless challenges of life.

Poona 1948: Talk #8, CW Vol. V, pp. 142-43

THE INTEGRATED HUMAN BEING

The professor had been teaching for many years, ever since he graduated from college, and had a large number of boys under him in one of the governmental institutions. He turned out students who could pass examinations, which was what the government and the parents wanted. Of course there were exceptional boys who were given special opportunities, granted scholarships and so on, but the vast majority were indifferent, dull, lazy, and somewhat mischievous. There were those who made something of themselves in whatever field they entered, but only very few had the creative flame. During all the years he had taught, the exceptional boys had been very rare; now and then there would be one who perhaps had the quality of genius, but it generally happened that he too was soon smothered by his environment. As a teacher he had visited many parts of the world to study this question of the exceptional boy, and everywhere it was the same. He was now withdrawing from the teaching profession, for after all these years he was rather saddened by the whole thing. However well boys were educated, on the whole they turned out to be a stupid lot. Some were clever or assertive and attained high positions, but behind the screen of their prestige and domination they were as petty and anxiety-ridden as the rest.

'The modern educational system is a failure,' he said, 'as it has produced two devastating wars and appalling misery. Learning to read and write and acquiring various techniques, which is the cultivation of memory, is obviously not enough, for it has produced unspeakable sorrow. What do you consider to be the end purpose of education?'

Is it not to bring about an integrated individual? If that is the purpose of education, then we must be clear as to whether the individual exists for society or whether society exists for the individual. If society needs and uses the individual for its own purposes, then it is not concerned with the cultivation of an integrated human being; what it wants is an efficient machine, a conforming and respectable citizen, and this requires only a very superficial integration. As long as the individual obeys and is willing to be thoroughly conditioned, society will find him useful and will spend time and money on him. But if society exists for the individual, then it must help in freeing him from its own conditioning influence. It must educate him to be an integrated human being.

'What do you mean by an integrated human being?'

To answer that question, one must approach it negatively, obliquely; one cannot consider its positive aspect.

'I don't understand what you mean.'

Positively to state what an integrated human being is only creates a pattern, a mould, an example, which we try to imitate; and is not the imitation of a pattern an indication of disintegration? When we try to copy an example, can there be integration? Imitation is a process of disintegration; and is this not what is happening in the world? We are all becoming very good gramophone records: we repeat what so-called religions have taught us, or what the latest political, economic or religious leader has said. We adhere to ideologies and attend political mass-meetings; there is mass-enjoyment of sport, mass-worship, mass-hypnosis. Is this a sign of integration? Conformity is not integration, is it? . . .

'What then is integration? I more or less understand what are the factors of disintegration, but that is only a negation. Through negation one cannot come to integration. I may know what is wrong, which does not mean that I know what is right.'

When the false is seen as the false, the true *is*. When one is aware of the factors of degeneration, not merely verbally but deeply, then is there not integration? Is integration static, something to be gained and finished with? Integration cannot be arrived at; arrival is death. It is not a goal, an end, but a state of being; it is a living thing, and how can a living thing be a goal, a purpose? The desire to be integrated is not different from any other desire, and all desire is a cause of conflict. When there is no conflict, there is integration. Integration is a state of complete attention. There cannot be complete attention if there is effort, conflict, resistance, concentration. Concentration is a fixation; concentration is a process of separation, exclusion, and complete attention is not possible when there is exclusion. To exclude is to narrow down, and the narrow can never be aware of the complete. Complete, full attention is not possible when there is condemnation, justification or identification, or when the mind is clouded by conclusions, speculations, theories. When we understand the hindrances, then only is there freedom. Freedom is an abstraction to the man in prison; but passive watchfulness uncovers the hindrances, and with freedom from these, integration comes into being.

Commentaries on Living: Series II, pp. 46-47 & 51

Questioner: I love my son. He may be killed in the war. What am I to do?

Krishnamurti: I wonder if you do love your son. If you really loved your son, would there be war? Would you not prevent war in any form if you really loved your son? Would you not bring about right education, an education which would not be identified with either the Orient or the Occident? If you really loved your son, would you not see to it that no belief divided human beings, that no national frontier stood between man and man?

I am afraid we do not love our children: *I love my son* is merely the accepted phrase. If we loved our sons, there would be a fundamental revolution in education, would there not? At the present time we are merely cultivating technique, efficiency. And the higher the efficiency, the greater the ruthlessness; the more nationalistic and separative we are, the faster society disintegrates. We are torn apart by our beliefs, by our ideologies, by our religions and dogmas; and inevitably there is conflict, not only between different societies but between groups in the same society.

So, although we may say that we love our children, we are obviously not deeply concerned about them as long as we are nationalistic, as long as we cling to our property, as long as we are bound, conditioned, by our religious beliefs. These are the disintegrating factors in society, leading inevitably to war and utter misery. If we are really desirous of saving the children, it is for us as individuals to bring about a fundamental transformation in ourselves. This means that we have to revalue the whole structure of society. That is a very complex and arduous business, and so we leave it to the experts, religious, economic and political. But the expert cannot understand that which is beyond his particular specialization. The specialist is never an integrated person, and integration is the only solution to our problem. There must be a total integration of ourselves as individuals, and only then can we educate the child to be an integrated human being. There obviously cannot be integration as long as there are racial, national, political and religious prejudices. Until we alter all that in ourselves fundamentally, we are bound to have war—and whatever you may say about loving your son is not going to stop it. What will stop war is the profound realization that one must oneself be free of those disintegrating factors which create war. It is only then that we will put an end to war. But unfortunately most of us are not interested in all this: we want an immediate result, an immediate answer. . . .

So, if we do love our children, then the structure of society will be fundamentally altered; and the more we love, the deeper will be our influence on society. Therefore it is important to understand the whole process of oneself, and no expert, no general, no teacher can give us the key to that understanding. Self-knowledge is the outcome of our own intensity, our own clarity, our own awareness in relationship; and relationship is not only with people but also with property and with ideas.

Seattle 1950: Talk #4, CW Vol. VI, pp. 236-37

THE INTEGRATED HUMAN BEING
(THE ROLE OF THE EDUCATOR)

What do we mean by education? Why do we want to be educated? Why do you send your children to be educated? Is it the mere acquisition of some technical knowledge which will give you a certain capacity with which to lead your life, so that you can apply that technique and get a profitable job? Is that what we mean by education—to pass certain examinations and then to become a clerk, and from a clerk to climb up the ladder of managerial efficiency? Or do we educate our children or educate ourselves in order to understand the whole complex problem of living? With what intention, actually, do we send our children to be educated or get educated ourselves? Taking it factually as things are, you get educated in order to get a job, and with that you are satisfied; and that is all you are concerned with, to be able to earn a livelihood by some means. So you go to a college or to a university, you soon marry and you have to earn a livelihood, and before you know where you are, you are a grandfather for the rest of your life. That is what most of us are doing with education. That is the fact. With that most of us are satisfied.

But is that education? Is that an integrating process in which there can be a comprehension of the whole, total process of life? That is, do you want to educate your children to understand the whole of life and not merely a segment of life like the physical, emotional, mental, psychological or spiritual; to have not the compartmental, divided outlook but a whole, total, integrated outlook on life in which, of course, there is the earning capacity? Now, which is it that we want, not theoretically but actually? What is our necessity? According to that, you will have universities, schools, examinations or no examinations. But to merely talk narrowly about linguistic divisions seems to me utterly infantile. What we will have to do as mature human beings—if such entities exist—is to go into this problem. Do you want your children to be educated to be glorified clerks, bureaucrats, leading utterly miserable, useless, futile lives, functioning as machines in a system? Or do you want integrated human beings who are intelligent, capable, fearless? We will find out, probably, what we mean by *intelligence*. The mere acquisition of knowledge is not intelligence, and it does not make an intelligent human being. You may have all the technique, but that does not necessarily mean that you are an intelligent, integrated human being.

So, what is this thing that brings about integration in life, that makes a human being intelligent? That is what we want; at least, that is what we intend to find out in our education, if we are at all intelligent and interested in education. That is what we are attempting to do, are we not? . . . Education is really one of our major problems, if not the most important problem in life, because everything is deteriorating around us and in us. We are not creative human beings: we are merely technicians. And if we are creating a new world, a new culture, surely there must be a revolution in our outlook on life and not merely the acceptance of things as they are, or the changing of things as they are.

Is it possible through education, the right kind of education, to bring about this integrated human being, that is, a human being who is thinking in terms of the whole and not merely of the part; who is thinking as a total entity, as a total process, and not indulging in divided, broken-up, fractional thinking? Is it possible for a human being to be intelligent—that is, to be without fear—through education, so that the mind is capable of thinking freely, not thinking in terms of a Hindu or a Muslim or a Christian or a communist? You can think freely only when your mind is unconditioned, that is, not conditioned as a Catholic or a communist and so on, so that you are capable of looking at all the influences of life which are constantly conditioning you; so that you are capable of examining, observing and freeing yourself from these conditions and influences; so that you are an intelligent human being without fear.

Our problem is how to bring about, through education, a human being who is creative, who is capable, who possesses that intelligence which is not burdened and which is not shaped in any particular direction, but is total; who is not belonging to any particular society, caste or religion, so that through that education and with that intelligence he arrives at maturity and therefore is capable of making his life not merely as a technician, but as a human being.

That is our problem, is it not? We see what is happening in the world, and especially in this industrially backward country: we are trying to catch up industrially with the rest of the world; we think it will take ourselves and our children to catch up with the rest of the world, so we are concerned with that and not with the whole total problem of living in which there is suffering, pain, death, the problem of sex, the whole problem of thinking, to live happily and creatively—we brush all that aside and are only concerned with special capacities. But we have to create a different human being, and so our whole educational system must undergo a revolution, which means really there must be the education of the educator; that is, the educator must himself be free or attempt to be free from all those qualities which are destructive in him, which are narrowing him down.

We must create a different human being who is creative. That is important, is it not? It is not possible to do this in a class where there are a hundred children or thirty or forty children and only one teacher. Which means, really, every teacher must have very few children; which means, again, the expense involved. So, seeing the complexities, the parents want to get their children educated somehow so that they may serve for the rest of their life in an office. But if you as parents really love your children—which I question—if you are really concerned with your children, if you are really interested in their education, you must understand this problem of what education is. It must present itself to you, must it not?

As things are at present, and with this educational system and the so-called passing of examinations, is it possible to bring about an integrated human being, a human being who understands life or who is struggling to understand life?—life being earning a livelihood, marriage, and all the problems of relationship, love, kindliness. This is only possible where there is no ambition. An ambitious man is not an intelligent man, he is a ruthless man; he may be ambitious spiritually but he is equally ruthless. Is it possible to have a human being without ambition? Can there be the right education which will produce such a human being, which means, really, a spiritual human being? I rather hesitate to use the word because you will immediately translate it in terms of some religious pursuit, some superstition, but if you are really concerned with education, is not that our problem?

Your immediate reaction to that is: you want to know the method, how this can be brought about. . . . Is there a method, a system for the educator which will bring about that state of integration in a human being? Or is there no method at all? Our educator must be much concerned, very watchful, very alert with each individual. As each individual is a living entity, the educator has to observe him, study him, and encourage in him that extraordinary quality of intelligence which will help him to become free, intelligent and fearless. Can there be a method to do that? Does not a method imply immediately conditioning a student to a particular pattern which you as educator think is important? You think you are helping him to grow into an intelligent human being by inflicting on him a pattern which you already have of what an intelligent human being should be. And you call that education and feel as though you have created a marvellous world, a world in which you are all kind, happy, creative.

We have not created a beautiful world, but perhaps if we know how to help the child to grow intelligently he might create a different world in which there will be no war, no antagonism between man and man. If you are interested in this, is it not the obvious responsibility of each grown-up individual to see that this kind of education does come about? Which means the educator can have only a very few students with him. There may be no examinations, but there will be the observation of each student and his capacities. This means that there will be no so-called mass-education, that is, educating thousands in two or three classes. That is not education.

So, if you are interested in this you will create a right kind of educator and help the child to be free to create a new world. It is not a one-man job; it is the responsibility of the educator, of the parent and of the student. It is not just the teacher alone that is responsible for creating a human being, intelligent and fearless, because the teacher may attempt it but when the child goes back home the people there will begin to corrupt him, they will begin to influence him, his family will begin to condition his mind. So it is a constant struggle. Unless you as parents cooperate with the teacher and produce the right kind of education, obviously there is going to be greater and greater deterioration. That is what intelligent human beings are concerned with: how to approach this problem. But most of you say you do not want to think of these problems at all; you want to be told what to do, to follow certain systems and put other things aside. All that you are concerned with is the begetting of children and passing them on to teachers.

If you were really concerned with the right type of education, it is your responsibility as grown-up people to see that through education there is right livelihood, not any old livelihood. Right livelihood implies, obviously, not joining the army, not becoming a policeman, not becoming a lawyer; those three professions are out if you are really concerned with the right kind of education. I know you laugh at it because it is a joke to you—it is an amazing thing—but if you really take it seriously you would not laugh. The world is destroying itself—there are more and more means of vast destruction of human beings—and those who laugh are not really concerned with the shadow of death which is constantly accompanying man.

One of the deteriorating factors for man is the wrong kind of education, as we have at present.

To create an intelligent human being there must be a complete revolution in our thinking. An intelligent human being means a fearless human being who is not bound by tradition, which does not mean he is immoral. You have to help your child to be free to find out, to create a new society—not a society according to a pattern such as Marxist, Catholic or capitalist. That requires a great deal of thought, concern and love, not mere discussions about love. If we really loved our children we would see that there would be right education.

Poona 1953: Talk #3, CW Vol. VII, pp. 157-60

BRAIN AND MIND

For most of us it is very difficult to see this, recognize it and do something about it, because we all think we are so terribly individual. We have identified ourselves with our bodies, with our reactions, with our nationalities, with our country. So we think we are individuals. Are we? Have you ever asked that question?—not superficially but basically, demanding the question whether you are actually an individual, which means indivisible. The meaning of *individual* is indivisible, not broken up, not fragmented. That is an individual. Are we? Or are we the result of a million years of collective experience, collective knowledge, collective belief and so on?

When you are asking this question, whether we are individuals at all—because our brains have evolved through time, accumulating a great deal of experience and knowledge—that brain, is it yours? Please ask this question of yourself. Don't, if one may request, identify yourself with it—then you cannot possibly ask the question. If you say, 'My brain is mine,' it is finished, all inquiry comes to an end. But if you are inquiring, if you are sensitively aware of the growth, of the evolution, from the micro to the present condition of the human brain, it has evolved through time, millions and millions of years—genetically, heredity, and all the rest of it—this brain is not ours, it is the brain of human beings. And that brain which is so extraordinarily capable—look what it has done in the field of technology, look what it has done in the field of nationalities, how it has invented gods, theories, saviours and so on—that brain operates with the instrument of thought. Thought is the instrument. Thought has created the techno- logical world, thought has created nationalities, thought has divided human beings—black, white, purple and all the rest of it. Thought has divided the religions—Christian, Hindu, Buddhist, Islam and so on. Thought has made this world in which we live, the technological world as well as the psycho- logical world. . . . Thought has created the marvellous cathe- drals, the churches, and also thought has created what is put in them: the rituals, the prayers, the symbols, as they are in India and all over the world. Thought is responsible for war, for Hiroshima, for the present condition of man's confusion, anxiety, uncertainty.

So, thought is part of this consciousness. Thought has put together the content of this consciousness. This is irrefutable. We are not doing any propagation of any particular idea, but we are together, *together now* becoming sensitively aware and looking very closely, without choice or identification, into the content of our own consciousness, of our own being. From there we act, from there we function, from there the self is created, the "me" that is our consciousness. Thought has put it there. When you say you are a Christian, believing in this or that, in the saviour and so on, thought is responsible for it. When you do any form of ritual, as in all religions . . . it is the result of thought. You may not like to hear all this, but these are facts. Thought is responsible. Thought has not created nature: the tree, the tiger, the heavens with their stars. But the astronauts can explore space—which is again the result of thought.

What is the thinker? It is the name, the form, and the brain that responds, is it not? This brain, through reactions and repeated stimuli, creates the mind. The mind is related to the brain, as the brain is related to the mind: they interact upon each other. But the mind is independent of the brain; and thought, though it depends on the brain, is also independent of it. I ask you where you live. You hear the question and a series of reactions take place in the brain, and then you remember where you live and tell me. . . . So, the brain creates the mind and the mind is related to the brain; there is an interaction going on all the time between the two. Yet the mind is independent, different from the brain; and it is the mind that is the centre of the "I", the thinker. It is this mind—which is the outcome of the brain—that thinks, 'I remember, my name is this, I live there, I have this job, I feel pain.' So, the thinking process is the result of the brain, and the thinking process creates the centre from which you say, 'I know, I don't know, I am happy, I am unhappy.' That centre is the bundle, the residue of all memory, of all experience, of all tradition, of the conscious as well as the unconscious. All that consciousness, which is the mind, is related to the brain. Between the two there is a constant interaction, and yet the mind, though related to it, is separate from the brain.

Ojai 1981: Talk #1, 2nd May

Questioner: How do you explain different levels of consciousness in terms of the human brain? The brain seems to be a physical affair; the mind does not seem to be a physical affair. In addition, the mind seems to have a conscious part and an unconscious part. How can we see with any clarity in all these different ideas?

Krishnamurti: What is the difference between the mind and the brain—is that it, sir? The actual physical brain which is the result of the past, which is the outcome of evolution, of many thousand yesterdays, with all its memories and knowledge and experience, is not that brain part of the total mind?—the mind in which there is the conscious and the unconscious level. The physical as well as the non-physical, the psychological, isn't all that one whole? Is it not we who have divided it as the conscious and the unconscious, the brain and the not-brain? Can we not look at the whole thing as a totality, non-fragmented?

Is the unconscious so very different from the conscious? Or is it not part of the totality, but we have divided it? From that arises the question: how is the conscious mind to be aware of the unconscious? Can the positive, which is the operative, the thing that is working all day, can that observe the unconscious?

The Flight of the Eagle, pp. 21-22

Krishnamurti: I think the mind is separate from the brain.

David Bohm: What does it mean, *separate?*

K: Separate in the sense, the brain is conditioned and the mind is not.

DB: Let's say the mind has a certain independence of the brain, is what you are saying. Even if the brain is conditioned . . .

K: . . . the other is not.

DB: It need not be . . .

K: . . . conditioned.

DB: On what basis do you say that?

K: No, let's not begin on what basis I say that.

DB: Well, what makes you say it?

K: As long as one's brain, or the brain, is conditioned it is not free.

DB: Yes.

K: And the mind is free.

DB: Yes, that is what you are saying. Now, the brain not being free means it is not free to inquire in an unbiased way.

K: I will go into it; let's inquire. What is freedom? Freedom to inquire, as you point out, freedom to investigate. And it is only in freedom there is deep insight.

DB: Yes, that's clear, because if you are not free to inquire or if you are biased, then you are limited, in an arbitrary way.

K: So as long as the brain is conditioned, its relationship to the mind is limited.

DB: Yes. Now we have the relationship of the brain to the mind, and also the other way round.

K: Yes. But the mind, being free, has a relationship to the brain.

DB: Yes. We say the mind is free in some sense, not subject to the conditioning of the brain.

K: Yes.

DB: What is the nature of the mind? Is the mind located inside the body or is it in the brain?

K: No, it is nothing to do with the body or the brain.

The Future of Humanity, pp. 57-58

KNOWLEDGE,
MEMORY, EXPERIENCE, THINKING

What is thought, what is thinking, what is the origin of the thinking process? . . . We are the entire humanity because our consciousness is not *my* consciousness; it is the consciousness that has evolved through time, through evolution, and has come to this present condition. Is there a possibility of totally understanding this consciousness and transforming it? That is why it is important to understand the nature of thought, because thought is the instrument of all our actions; it is thought that has put together all the content of our consciousness: our beliefs, our ideas, our hopes, our aspirations, our fears, anxieties, loneliness, depression . . .

The whole world is emphasizing thinking, the whole world is acquiring more and more knowledge. Psychologically and outwardly, knowledge has become all-important. And what is knowledge?—scientific knowledge, business knowledge, the knowledge of music, composition. There are the scholars and scientists who say that through knowledge alone man ascends, grows, becomes. . . . Knowledge can never be complete about anything. Knowledge means accumulation of experience, of tradition, gathering all kinds of information which has been stored up, learning about it, and having a degree and functioning . . . Knowledge has become extraordinarily important. . . . Our thought can never be complete because knowledge comes through experience, and you store up that experience as knowledge which then is held in the brain as memory, and that memory acts, which is thinking. . . .

So, thought born of knowledge, born of experience, stored in the brain as memory, the remembrance of things past—that is thought. And so thought in itself is fragmentary. It is not my thinking and your thinking, separate: there is only thinking. . . . Thinking is common to all of us. Whether you are very poor, highly educated or totally ignorant, thinking is going on. So, thought is the origin . . . of this division in our life. . . . Thought seeks security in isolation because it is fragmented; it is the process of its own division.

Saanen 1982: Talk #2, 13ᵗʰ July

The central problem of our existence is thought, the whole machinery of thinking, and our civilization both in the East and in the West is based on thought, on the intellect. Thought is very limited, it is measurable, and thought has done the most extraordinary things in the world: the whole technological world, going to the moon . . . But thought has done a great deal of mischief: all the instruments of war, the destruction of nature, the pollution of the earth. If one goes into it very deeply, thought has created the so-called religions throughout the world. . . . Thought has created . . . an extraordinary world: the marvellous cities, which are decaying, the quick transportation, and all that. And thought has divided human beings in their relationship. Thought, which is the response of memory, experience, knowledge, divides human beings. In our relationship with each other, thought has built through a series of incidents and activities, the image of the "me" and the "you". . . . These images are mechanistic, and therefore relationship becomes mechanical. So, there is not only the division brought about by thought in the outside world but also there is division in the human being inwardly. . . .

Thinking is the response of memory, experience, knowledge, which is the past. Thought projects the future through the present, modifying it, shaping it, designing it as the future. So, thought has a logical function, efficient, if it is not personal; then there is the accumulated knowledge of science and all the accumulation of ideas. . . . But knowledge . . . prevents the mind going beyond the present and the past. Thought can only function in the field of the known, though it may label the unknown according to its conditioning, to its knowledge of the known, and project the unknown. And you observe this phenomenon right through the world: the ideal, the future, the *what should be* . . . according to the background, to the conditioning, to the education, to the environment. Thought is also responsible for behaviour—the vulgarity, the crudeness, the brutality, the violence in all relationships, and so on. And so thought is measurable.

I do not know if you have noticed . . . that the West is the explosion of Greece, which thought in terms of measure. . . . To them mathematics, logic, philosophy . . . is the result of measurement, which is thought. Does this interest you? . . . Because without understanding the whole machinery of thought, what its tremendous significance is, and where it becomes utterly destructive, meditation has no meaning. So, unless you really understand, have a deep insight into the whole machinery of thinking, you cannot possibly go beyond it. . . .

The ancient Indians said measurement is illusion, because when you can measure something it is very limited, and if you base all your structure, all your morality, all your existence on measurement, which is thought, then you can never be free; therefore they said . . . that the immeasurable is the real and the measurable is the unreal, which they call *maya*.

So, what is thinking? I want to be very clear in myself, and therefore with you, to find out what thinking is, to discover or to find out its right place. We said thinking is the response of memory, experience, knowledge stored up in the brain cells; therefore thought is the result of development, evolution, which is time. So thought is the result of time. . . . Thought can only function within the space it creates around itself. And that space is very limited; that space is the "me" and the "you". Thought, the whole machinery of thinking, has a rightful place, and thought in relationship between two human beings becomes destructive. . . .

So, knowledge is absolutely essential. You can add to it, take away from it . . . but the immensity of knowledge is a human necessity. Is knowledge necessary in relationship between human beings? . . . What place has thought in relationship—thought which is capable of remembering, imagining, contriving, designing, calculating—what place has it in human relationship? Has it any place, or no place at all?

What is the place of thought in existence? For now . . . all our existence is based on thought, which may imagine it is not based on it, that it is based on some spiritual substance, but it is still the product of thought. Our gods, our saviours, our masters, our gurus are the product of thought. What place has thought in life, in existence? It has its place logically, sanely, effectively when knowledge functions without the interference of the "me" who is using knowledge, who says, 'I am a better scientist than that person,' 'I am a better guru than that guru.' So, knowledge when used without the "me" which is the product of thought, which creates the division between "me" and "you" . . . is the most extraordinary thing because that will bring about a better world, a better structure of the world, a better society. We have enough knowledge to bring about a happy world where we can all have food, clothing, shelter, vocation, no ghettos; but that is denied because thought has separated itself as the "me" and the "you", my country and your country, my beastly god and your beastly god, and we are at war with each other.

Saanen 1972: Talk #3, 20th July

Our consciousness is put together by thought. Thought dominates all our activities: thought has constructed the atom bomb, the marvellous cathedrals and the things that are in them; thought has created all the travail, all the problems that we have. . . . Thought is responsible for fear, for anxiety, for sorrow, for the pursuit of happiness and the pursuit of what is called God, enlightenment—it is all the movement of thought. . . . Thought has invented all the religions, all the content of the religions—the rituals, the dogmas, the beliefs, the hierarchical outlook of a religious mind—all the product of thought, there is no denying that. . . .

Our brains are trained to solve problems, whether the problems be scientific, engineering, social, religious and so on. . . . The brain is the movement of thought, and we are only using a small part of the brain. The specialist will tell you this too, that we are not employing the whole of the brain but only a small part of it. And the part is conditioned by time, which is evolution, by experience, by knowledge—that part has been trained to solve problems, which thought has created. See what the brain is doing: first it has been educated to act partially, and that partiality is the result of partial thinking. Thinking is limited because it is based on knowledge, on experience and on memory, and knowledge can never be complete about anything; and so our thinking is limited. That thinking creates the problems, and our brains are trained to solve the problems which thought has created, so it is caught in a cycle. . . . And in trying to solve the problem, it becomes more and more complicated, which is what is happening in the world. The politicians are trying to solve problems, but they are increasing them. Like the gurus who want to solve problems, they are again multiplying them. This is happening. . . .

So, we come back to the question: if thought is not capable of solving all these . . . human problems, the problems of relationship with each other, the problem that thought creates images, the problems of fear, sorrow, meditation, all that; if thought cannot resolve all these problems, which apparently it cannot after all these millennia, we must look in other directions, not pursue the same old traditional path. Are we prepared for that? . . . Do we see that there must be a totally different approach to the whole problem of existence, whether it is sexual, religious, sensory, and all the rest of it? How will you find out a totally different approach which is not contaminated by thought, because one realizes thought is utterly limited? The problems which thought has created are much too great, and thought cannot solve them anymore. If one actually, not intellectually nor emotionally but actually realizes it as you realize pain, if one is passionately aware of it, then what is the other direction?

Brockwood Park 1981: Talk #1, 29th August

THOUGHT PROCESS, EGO PROCESS

To understand relationship, to see very clearly in relationship the fact of what you are, there must be no condemnation or justification: you must look at the fact with freedom. How can you understand something if you condemn it or wish it to be something other than it is? Through your understanding of relationship there comes the discovery from minute to minute of the ways of your thinking, the structure of your mind. As long as the mind does not understand its total process, both the conscious and the unconscious, there can be no freedom. So, through the relationship of everyday contacts, of everyday action, you come to a point when you see that the thinker is not different from thought. When you say the *atman* is different from the ego, it is still within the field of thought; and without understanding the process, the functioning of thought, it is utterly futile to talk of reality and the *atman* because they have no existence: they are merely the prejudices of thought. What we have to do is to understand the thought process, and that can be understood only in relationship. Self-knowledge begins with the understanding of relationship.

Bombay 1950: Talk #1, CW Vol. VI, p. 91

Relationship can only exist when there is total abandonment of the self, the "me". When the "me" is not, then you are related; in that there is no separation whatsoever. Probably one has not felt that, the total denial—not intellectually but actually—the total cessation of the "me". Perhaps that's what most of us are seeking, sexually or through identification with something greater. But that process of identification with something greater is the product of thought; and thought is old—like the "me", the ego, the "I", it is of yesterday, it is always old. The question then arises: how is it possible to let go this isolating process completely, this process which is centred in the "me"? How is this to be done? How am I, whose activity of everyday life is of fear, anxiety, despair, sorrow, confusion and hope; how is the "me" which separates itself from another—through identification with God, with its conditioning, with its society, with its social and moral activity, with the State and so on—how is that to die, to disappear, so that the human being can be related? Because if we are not related then we are going to live at war with each other. . . . How can we live so that there is no separation, so that we can really cooperate?

There is so much to do in the world: to wipe away poverty, to live happily, to live with delight instead of with agony and fear, to build a totally different kind of society, a morality which is above all morality. But this can only be when the morality of present-day society is totally denied. There is so much to do, and it cannot be done if there is this constant isolating process going on. We speak of the "me" and the "mine" and the "other". The "other" is beyond the wall, the "me" and the "mine" is this side of the wall. So, how can that essence of resistance which is the "me", how can that be completely let go? That is really the most fundamental question in all relationship. . . .

Talks in Europe 1968, Paris: Talk #4

IDENTITY AND IDENTIFICATION

W hy do you identify yourself with another, with a group, with a country? Why do you call yourself a Christian, a Hindu, a Buddhist, or why do you belong to one of the innumerable sects? Religiously and politically one identifies oneself with this or that group through tradition or habit, through impulse, prejudice, imitation and laziness. This identification puts an end to all creative understanding and then becomes a mere tool in the hands of the party boss, the priest, or the favoured leader. . . .

When we identify ourselves with another, is that an indication of love? Does identification imply experimentation? Does not identification put an end to love and to experiment? Identification is possession, the assertion of ownership; and ownership denies love. To own is to be secure; possession is defence, making oneself invulnerable. In identification there is resistance, whether gross or subtle; and is love a form of self-protective resistance? . . .

Identification is essentially a thought process by which the mind safeguards and expands itself; and in becoming something it must resist and defend, it must own and discard. In this process of becoming, the mind or the self grows tougher and more capable; but this is not love. Identification destroys freedom, and only in freedom can there be the highest form of sensitivity . . .

Does not the very act of identification put an end to inquiry, to discovery? The happiness that truth brings cannot be if there is no experimentation in self-discovery. Identification puts an end to discovery; it is another form of laziness. Identification is vicarious experience, and hence utterly false.

To experience, all identification must cease. To experiment there must be no fear. Fear prevents experience. It is fear that makes for identification—identification with another, with a group, with an ideology, and so on. Fear must resist, suppress; and in a state of self-defence how can there be venturing on the uncharted sea? Truth or happiness cannot come without undertaking the journey into the ways of the self. You cannot travel far if you are anchored. Identification is a refuge. A refuge needs protection, and that which is protected is soon destroyed. Identification brings destruction upon itself, and hence the constant conflict between various identifications.

The more we struggle for or against identification, the greater is the resistance to understanding. If one is aware of the whole process of identification, outward as well as inner, if one sees that its outward expression is projected by the inner demand, then there is a possibility of discovery and happiness. He who has identified himself can never know freedom, in which alone all truth comes into being.

Commentaries on Living: Series I, pp. 11-13

Questioner: How can individual regeneration alone possibly bring about, in the immediate, the collective wellbeing of the greatest number, which is the need everywhere?

Krishnamurti: We think that individual regeneration is opposed to collective regeneration. . . . Regeneration is anonymous: it is not, 'I have redeemed myself.' As long as you think of individual regeneration as being opposed to the collective, then there is no relationship between the two. But if you are concerned with regeneration not of the individual, but *regeneration,* then you will see there is quite a different force—intelligence—at work . . .

Intelligence is not yours or mine: it is intelligence. I think it is important to see this deeply. Then our political and individual action, collective or otherwise, will be quite different. We shall lose our identity; we shall not identify ourselves with something: our country, our race, our group, our collective traditions, our prejudices. We shall lose all those things because the problem demands that we shall lose our identity in order to solve it. But that requires great, comprehensive understanding of the whole problem.

Our problem is not the bread-and-butter problem alone; our problem is not feeding, clothing and shelter alone, it is more profound than that. It is a psychological problem: why man identifies himself. It is this identification—with a party, with a religion, with knowledge—that is dividing us. That identity can be resolved only when, psychologically, the whole process of identifying, the desire, the motive, is clearly understood.

So, the problem of the collective or of the individual is non-existent when you are pursuing the solution of a particular problem. If you and I are both interested in something, vitally interested in the solution of the problem, we shall not identify ourselves with something else. But unfortunately, as we are not vitally interested, we have identified ourselves, and it is that identity that is preventing us from resolving this complex and vast problem.

Madras 1952: Talk #8, CW Vol. VI, pp. 296-97

We must re-educate ourselves not to murder, not to liquidate each other for any cause, however righteous it may appear to be for the future happiness of mankind, for an ideology, however promising—not merely be educated technically, which inevitably makes for ruthlessness, but to be content with little, to be compassionate, and to seek the supreme.

The prevention of this ever-increasing destruction and horror depends on each one of us—not on any organization or planning, not on any ideology, not on the invention of greater instruments of destruction, not on any leader, but on each one of us. Do not think that wars cannot be stopped by so humble and lowly a beginning. A stone may alter the course of a river. To go far, you must begin near. To understand the world chaos and misery, you must comprehend your own confusion and sorrow, for out of these come the magnified issues of the world. To understand yourself, there must be constant meditative awareness which will bring to the surface the causes of violence and hate, greed and ambition, and by studying them without identification, thought will transcend them. For none can lead you to peace save yourself: there is no leader, no system that can bring war, exploitation, oppression to an end save yourself. Only by your thoughtfulness, by your compassion, by your awakened understanding can there be established goodwill and peace.

Ojai 1944: Talk #10, CW Vol. III, pp. 242-43

CONCENTRATION, AWARENESS AND ATTENTION

Questioner: For most of us, the act of attention is difficult to maintain. Only a small part of one is willing, seriously interested. What can one do to nourish this attention?

Krishnamurti: What do we mean by attention? What is the difference between awareness, concentration and attention? Could we go into that together? As one is sitting under these beautiful trees on a lovely morning, nice and cool, one is aware of that woodpecker pecking away; one is aware of the green lawn, the beautiful trees, the spotted sunlight and those mountains. How does one look at them? How do you look at this marvellous sight and the beauty of this place? What does it mean to you? Are you aware of it without any choice, without any desire—do you just observe the extraordinary beauty of the land? When you so observe the light and the shade, the branches, the dark trunks, and the light on the leaf, and the extension of this marvellous earth, how do you react to all that? What is the feeling behind that awareness? The beauty of the land and the hills and the shadows, is it related to our life, is it part of our life? . . . What is its relationship to our life? That is part of awareness—the awareness of the external and the awareness of one's own reactions to the external—to be aware of this movement. As you are sitting there, are you aware of the colours of the shirts and the dresses—are you aware of all that?

Or when we are aware, is there always a choice?—I prefer this land to another land, I prefer this valley to other valleys—so there is always memory and choice operating. Can one be aware without any choice at all—be aware of the extraordinary sense of the blue sky through the leaves—and just move with it all? Is one aware of one's reactions, and when one is aware of one's reactions, is there a preference?— one is more desirable than the other, one is more urgent than the other, one is more continuous, habitual, and so on. And so from the outer move to the inner, so that there is no division between the outer and the inner: it's like a tide going out and coming in. There is an awareness of the world outside of us and an awareness of the world inside of us, the conscious as well as the unconscious. When one is really deeply aware, there is no remnant or hidden, unconscious movement.

So, awareness is this movement of the outer and the inner, and to discover for oneself whether there is a division between the outer and the inner. Of course there is a division between the tree and myself: I am not the tree, I hope. But in observing that thing which we call *tree,* to discover our reactions to it; how we react to beauty and quietness, to ugliness, to brutality, to violence, and so on.

What do we mean by concentration? Because they are all related: awareness, concentration and attention. What is concentration? To concentrate upon a page, upon a picture; to concentrate all one's energy on a particular point. In that concentration, is there not the effort to concentrate? That is, you are trying to read a particular page and out of the window you see a marvellous light on a flower, and your thought wanders off to that; then you try to pull that thought back and concentrate on something. So there is resistance, a constant struggle to focus one's energy, visually and so on, all the time trying to focus on a particular point.

The questioner says that attention happens occasionally, and how is one to nourish that attention so that it is continuous, not haphazard? So we are asking what attention is. To attend to that woodpecker. Did you listen to that woodpecker? There it is!

In concentration there is always the one who tries to concentrate, and in that concentration there is effort and control; there is the controller who is trying to focus his thought on a particular subject. But thought is all the time moving, wandering around, so he tries to control it. In that control there is a form of resistance; there is a division between the controller and the controlled. Where there is division there must be conflict, between the controller and the controlled.

In attention, is there this division?—the controller trying to attend and therefore a division between the controller and the thought that says, I must attend, I must learn how to sustain attention or nourish it. Is there in attention a centre from which you attend? Or when you listen to that woodpecker, you are *listening*. Is there in attention an entity who is attending, or is there only attention? Which means attending with your listening, perception, seeing, and giving all your energy to attend to something. . . . When you really listen, there is no centre as the "me" who is listening; whereas in concentration there is always a centre. Attention has no centre and it cannot be nourished. You attend if you are listening, if there is intensity. Attention has no periphery, whereas concentration has: it is limited.

Ojai 1982: Q&A #2, 6th May

To be choicelessly aware of the total process of the unconscious as well as the conscious, there must be a negative state of mind. I think it is fairly clear what I mean by a *negative state of mind.* The positive state is that of condemning, judging, evaluating, approving, denying, agreeing or disagreeing, and it is the result of your particular conditioning. But the negative approach is not the opposite of the positive.

If you wish to understand what the speaker is saying, you have to listen negatively. To listen negatively is not to accept or reject what he is saying, or compare it with what is said in the Bible, or with what your analyst says—you just listen. In that state of negative listening, you are aware of your own reactions without judging them; therefore you begin to understand yourself, not just what the speaker is saying. What the speaker is saying is only a mirror in which you are looking at yourself.

This awareness implies attention, does it not? And in the state of attention there is no effort to concentrate. The moment you say you must concentrate, you have engendered conflict because such concentration implies contradiction. You want to concentrate on something but your thought wanders away, so you try to pull it back, and you keep this battle going. When this battle is going on you are not listening. If you go into it a little, you will find that what is being said is an actual fact; it is not a thing to be applied to yourself because you have heard somebody say something about it.

So, awareness is a state of choiceless attention. Without this awareness, this choiceless attention, to talk about what is beyond, what is the timeless and so on, has no meaning whatsoever. That is mere speculation. It is like sitting at the foot of a hill and asking somebody what is beyond it. To find out, you have to climb the hill. But nobody wants to climb the hill; at least, very few want to. Most of us are satisfied with explanations, with concepts, with ideas, with symbols. We try to understand merely verbally what attention is, what awareness is. But this understanding of oneself is quite an arduous task. I am using that word *arduous* not in the sense of a conflict or an effort to achieve something. One has to be really interested in all this. If you are not interested, it is all right, you can just leave it alone. But if you are interested, you will find it arduous to pursue the understanding of yourself to the very end. All human problems arise from this extraordinarily complex, living centre which is the "me", and a man who would uncover its subtle ways has to be negatively aware, choicelessly observant. Any effort to see, any form of compulsion, distorts what is seen, and therefore there is no seeing at all.

London 1962: Talk #6, CW Vol. XIII, pp. 201-02

LISTENING, LOOKING, LEARNING

I f one listens . . . without effort, with clarity, then that very listening is the vehicle of action. You do not have to do anything about it: the very act of listening is action. It is like seeing something, it is like looking at a flower. We never actually look at a flower because we look with our minds, with our thoughts, with our ideas, opinions, with our botanical knowledge of that flower. So it is thought that looks—not so much the eye as thought. Our thoughts, ideas, opinions, judgements, knowledge, these interfere with our looking. It is only when you can look at something completely that you are in direct contact with that thing; and to look completely demands a great deal of energy, not words, words, words— they don't create energy. What brings energy is this observing, listening, learning in which there is not the observer; there is only the fact, and not the experiencer looking at the fact.

Paris 1965: Talk #1, CW Vol. XV, p.155

A boy in a class wants to look out of the window. A bird is flying by, there is a lovely flower on the tree, or someone goes by. His attention is taken away from the book and the teacher tells him to concentrate on the book. That is how most of our life is. We want to look, but society, economy, religious doctrines force us to conform, and therefore we lose all spontaneity, all freshness. The discipline of learning is something entirely different from the discipline of acquiring knowledge. You need to have a certain discipline when you are acquiring technological knowledge or any other knowledge. You have to pay attention, give your mind to something particular, to specialize in a subject, and that entails a certain discipline of conformity, of suppression, and all the things that are happening in the world through discipline. The discipline which we are talking about has nothing whatsoever to do with the discipline of conformity to a pattern. . . . We are learning, and that learning is never conformity to a pattern—how can it be? Whether the pattern has been laid down by the Buddha, by Christ, by Shankara, or by your own pet guru, learning has nothing whatever to do with it. Because in that conformity all learning ceases and therefore there is never originality. We are discovering through learning, with originality. I do not know whether you see the beauty of what we are talking about. Watching, looking, seeing, listening are all parts of learning. If you do not know how to listen, you cannot learn. If you do not know how to see a flower, you cannot learn about the beauty of that flower. And to listen, to see, to learn implies in itself a discipline which is not conformity.

New Delhi 1964: Talk #3, CW Vol. XIV, p. 240

FREEDOM

Revolt is not freedom. Revolt is still within the pattern of society, and freedom is outside the pattern of society. The pattern or mould of society is psychological; it is the envy, greed, ambition, the various conflicts of which we are a part. We are the society which we have made; and if one is not free from it, there cannot possibly be order. So, virtue is of the highest importance because it brings freedom. And one must be free—but that is what most people don't want. They may want political freedom—freedom to vote for some politician, or nationalistic freedom—but that is not freedom at all.

Freedom is something entirely different. Most of us do not want freedom inwardly, in the deep sense of that word, because it implies that we must stand completely alone, without a guide, without a system, without following any authority; and that requires enormous order within oneself. Most of us want to lean on somebody, and if it's not a person then it's an idea, a belief, a way of conduct, a pattern established by society or by some leader or so-called spiritual person. . . .

A man who seeks truth has no authority of any kind, at any time, and this freedom from authority is one of the most difficult things for most of us to grasp, not only in the Western world but also in the East, because we think that somebody else will bring about order in our life—a saviour, a master, a spiritual teacher—which is absolutely absurd. It is only through our own clarity, through our own investigation, awareness, attention, that we begin to learn all about ourselves; and out of that learning, out of that understanding of ourselves, come freedom and order.

Paris 1965: Talk #4, 27th May

Learning about oneself and accumulating knowledge about oneself are two different things. Please . . . do not merely accept what I am saying, but we are investigating, discovering together. We are taking a journey together, and therefore you are as much aware as the speaker, you are working as hard as the speaker, which means that we are both inquiring together. So, to come upon this freedom, this silence and space, one must negate the whole psychological structure of society in which one is. That is extraordinarily interesting and important, for otherwise one functions merely mechanically; and to deny the whole psychological structure of society, which we have made and of which we are a part, requires attention, observing ourselves as we are every day. In this total awareness is the realisation of that which actuality *is*, and in that there is freedom.

Paris 1967: Talk #4, 27th April

Life is a thing which is living, constantly moving. We recreate according to our memory and are not capable of adjusting to the immediate demands of life, so we approach reality, which is living, which is a very complex process, with a mind that is already burdened with knowledge, with experience, with ideas. A mind which is always meeting life with memory is not free. And religious revolution is the freeing of action from memory. After all, the "me", the ego, the self, is the accumulation of various experiences, of knowledge, of memory. The "me" is nothing but background, the "me" is of time; the self, the ego is the result of various forms of accumulated knowledge, information. It is that bundle which we call "I". The "I" is the many layers of memory. Though the "I" may be unconscious of the many layers, it is still part of the known. So, when I seek, I am only seeking that which I know. That which I know is the projection from my past, and it is the freedom from the known that is the real revolution.

I cannot be free through any discipline, through any practice, because I am a bundle of memory, experiences, knowledge; and if I practise a discipline to free my mind from the "I", it is merely another continuance of memory. So, there is no freedom from the "me", the known, whether you are conscious or unconscious of it. That freedom can only come about when there is the understanding of the whole process of the "me"—not to direct the process, because in the "me", when it directs, there is the director and also the thing it directs, which are both the same. There is no observer different from the observed: there is only one entity, the experiencer and the experienced. As long as there is the experiencer, which is the "me" experiencing something wanted, it is still the known. So our difficulty is, is it not, that our mind is always moving from the known to the known. How is this movement to be stopped? . . .

Creativity is the action of the unknown, not of the known. The unknown is truth, God. The activity of that state, of that reality, is creative; it is the action without memory. That is why I feel it is astonishingly, immensely important to find out not *how* to free the mind from the known, but to be in that state when the mind is free from the known. The being of the freedom from the known is the true religious revolution.

Bombay 1954: Talk 4, CW Vol. VIII p. 183

FREEDOM AND ORDER IN SCHOOL

Krishnamurti: You cannot have freedom merely for the asking; you cannot say, 'I will be free to do what I like,' because there are other people also wanting to be free, also wanting to express what they feel, also wanting to do what they wish. Everybody wants to be free and yet they want to express themselves—their anger, their brutality, their ambition, their competitiveness, and so on. So there is always conflict. I want to do something and you want to do something and so we fight. Freedom is not doing what one wants, because man cannot live by himself. Even the monk, even the *sannyasi,* is not free to do what he wants because he has to struggle for what he wants, to fight with himself, to argue within himself. It requires enormous intelligence, sensitivity, understanding to be free. And yet it is absolutely necessary that every human being, whatever his culture, be free. So, you see, freedom cannot exist without order.

Student: Do you mean that to be free, there should be no discipline?

K: . . . You cannot have freedom without order, and order is discipline. I do not like to use that word *discipline* because it is laden with all kinds of meaning. Discipline means conformity, imitation, obedience; it means to do what you are told, doesn't it? But if you want to be free—and human beings must be completely free, otherwise they cannot flower, otherwise they cannot be real human beings—you have to find out for yourself what it is to be orderly, what it is to be punctual, kind, generous, unafraid. The discovery of all that is discipline. This brings about order. To find out, you have to examine, and to examine you must be free. If you are considerate, if you are watching, if you are listening, then because you are free you will be punctual, you will come to the class regularly, you will study, you will be so alive that you will want to do things rightly.

S: You say that freedom is very dangerous to man. Why is it so?

K: Why is freedom dangerous? You know what society is?

S: It is a big group of people which tells you what to do and what not to do.

K: It is a big group of people which tells you what to do and what not to do. It is also the culture, the customs, the habits of a certain community; the social, moral, ethical, religious structure in which man lives—that is generally called society. Now, if each individual in that society did what he liked, he would be a danger to that society. If you did what you liked here in the school, what would happen? You would be a danger to the rest of the school, wouldn't you? So, people do not generally want others to be free. A man who is really free, not in ideas, but inwardly free from greed, ambition, envy, cruelty, is considered a danger to people because he is entirely different from the ordinary man. So, society either worships him or kills him or is indifferent to him.

S: You said that we must have freedom and order, but how are we to get it?

K: First of all, you cannot depend on others; you cannot expect somebody to give you freedom and order—whether it is your father, your mother, your husband, your teacher. You have to bring it about in yourself. This is the first thing to realize: that you cannot ask anything from another except food, clothes and shelter. You cannot possibly ask or look to anyone, your gurus or your gods. Nobody can give you freedom and order. So, you have to find out how to bring about order in yourself, that is, you have to watch and find out for yourself what it means to bring about virtue in yourself. Do you know what virtue is: to be moral, to be good? Virtue is order. So, find out in yourself how to be good, how to be kind, how to be considerate. And out of that consideration, out of that watching, you bring about order and therefore freedom. You depend on others to tell you what you should do: that you should not look out of the window, that you should be punctual, that you should be kind. But if you were to say, 'I will look out of the window when I want to look, but when I study I am going to look at the book,' you bring order within yourself, without being told by others.

S: What does one gain by being free?

K: Nothing. When you talk about what one gains, you are really thinking in terms of merchandise, are you not? I will do this and in return for it please give me something. I am kind to you because it is profitable for me. But that is not kindliness. So, as long as we are thinking in terms of gaining something, there is no freedom. If you say, 'If I get freedom I will be able to do this and that,' then it is not freedom. So do not think in terms of utility. As long as we are thinking in terms of using, there is no question of freedom at all. Freedom can only exist when there is no motive. You do not love somebody because they give you food, clothes or shelter. Then it is not love.

Do you ever walk by yourself? Or do you always go with others? If you go out by yourself sometimes, not too far away because you are very young, then you will get to know yourself: what you think, what you feel, what is virtue, what you want to be. Find out. And you cannot find out about yourself if you are always talking, going about with your friends, with half a dozen people. Sit under a tree, quietly by yourself, not with a book. Just look at the stars, the clear sky, the birds, the shape of the leaves. Watch the shadow, watch the bird across the sky. By being with yourself, you begin to understand the workings of your own mind, and that is as important as going to class.

Krishnamurti on Education, pp. 30-33

FEAR AND AUTHORITY IN SCHOOL

What place has authority in a school? We have to study authority, not merely assert that there should be no authority but only freedom. We have to study it as we study the atom. The structure of the atom is orderly. Obedience, following, accepting authority, whether it is blind or clear-eyed, must inevitably bring about disorder. What is the root of obedience, which breeds authority? When one is in disorder, confusion, society becomes utterly chaotic; then that very disorder creates authority, as has happened so often historically. Is fear the root of accepting authority, being uncertain, without clarity in oneself? Then each human being helps to bring about the authority that will tell us what to do, as has happened in all religions, all sects and communities. It is the everlasting problem of the guru and the disciple, each destroying the other. The follower then becomes the leader. This cycle is forever repeating itself.

We are studying together, in the real sense of the word, what the cause of authority is. If each one of us sees that it is fear, muddle-headedness, or some deeper factor, then the mutual study of it, verbal or non-verbal, has significance. In studying, there may be an exchange of thought and the silent observation of the cause of authority. Then that very study uncovers the light of intelligence, for intelligence has no authority. It is not your intelligence or my intelligence. A few of us may see this deeply, without any deception, and it is our responsibility that this flame be spread wherever we are, in school, at home, or in a bureaucratic government. It has no abiding place; it is wherever you are.

The Whole Movement of Life is Learning, p. 173

Should you not have this quality of real affection: to be considerate naturally, without enforcement, without motive? Real affection cannot be brought into being artificially, you have to feel it; and your guardian, your parents, your teachers must also feel it. Most people have no real affection; they are too concerned with their achievements, their longings, their knowledge, their success. They give to what they have done and want to do such colossal importance that it ultimately destroys them.

That is why it is very important, while you are young, to help look after the rooms, or to care for a number of trees which you yourself have planted, or to go to the assistance of a sick friend, so that there is a subtle feeling of sympathy, of concern, of generosity—real generosity which is not just of the mind and which makes you want to share with somebody whatever you may have, however little. If you do not have this feeling of love, of generosity, of kindness, of gentleness while you are young, it will be very difficult to have it when you are older; but if you begin to have it now, then perhaps you can awaken it in others.

To have sympathy and affection implies freedom from fear. But you see, it is very difficult to grow up in this world without fear, without having some personal motive in action. The older people have never thought about this problem of fear, or they have thought about it only abstractly, without acting upon it in daily existence. You are still very young, you are watching, inquiring, learning; but if you do not see and understand what causes fear, you will become as they are. Like some hidden weed, fear will grow and spread and twist your mind. You should therefore be aware of everything that is happening around you and within yourself—how the teachers talk, how your parents behave and how you respond—so that this question of fear is seen and understood.

Most grown-up people think that some kind of discipline is necessary. Do you know what discipline is? It is a process of making you do something which you do not want to do. Where there is discipline there is fear. So, discipline is not the way of love. That is why discipline at all costs should be avoided—discipline being coercion, resistance, compulsion, making you do something which you really do not understand, or persuading you to do it by offering you a reward. If you don't understand something, don't do it, and don't be compelled to do it. Ask for an explanation. Don't just be obstinate, but try to find out the truth of the matter so that no fear is involved and your mind becomes very pliable, very supple.

When you do not understand and are merely compelled by the authority of grown-up people, you are suppressing your own mind and then fear comes into being, and that fear pursues you like a shadow throughout life. That is why it is so important not to be disciplined according to any particular type of thought or pattern of action. But most older people can think only in those terms. They want to make you do something for your so-called good. This very process of making you do something for your own good destroys your sensitivity, your capacity to understand, and therefore your love. To refuse to be coerced or compelled is very difficult because the world about us is so strong; but if we merely give in and do things without understanding, we fall into a habit of thoughtlessness, and then it becomes still more difficult for us to break away.

So, in your school should you have authority, discipline? Or should you be encouraged by your teachers to discuss these questions, go into them, understand them so that, when you are grown up and go out into the world, you will be a mature human being who is capable of meeting intelligently the world's problems? You cannot have that deep intelligence if there is any kind of fear. Fear only makes you dull; it curbs your initiative, it destroys that flame which we call sympathy, generosity, affection, love. So, do not allow yourself to be disciplined into a pattern of action, but find out, which means that you must have the time to question, to inquire. And the teachers must also have the time; if there is no time, then time must be made. Fear is a source of corruption, it is the beginning of degeneration, and to be free of fear is more important than any examination or any scholastic degree.

Life Ahead, pp. 95-97

INSIGHT

Pupul Jayakar: What is the nature of the ground from which insight springs?

Krishnamurti: Insight can take place only when there is freedom from time and thought.

PJ: It is a sort of unending . . .

K: No, it is not. You are complicating a very simple fact, as most of us do. To live in peace is to flower, it is to understand the extraordinary world of peace. Peace cannot be brought about by thought.

PJ: Please understand, Krishnaji, it is the brain itself which listens to that statement.

K: Yes, it listens. And then what happens? If it listens, it is quiet. It is not ruminating, it is not going on: 'By Jove, what does he mean?' It is not rattling; it is quiet.

PJ: Yes, it is quiet.

K: When it is actually quiet, not induced quietness, when it actually listens and there is quietness, then there is insight. I don't have to explain in ten different ways the limitation of thought; it is so.

PJ: I see what you're saying. Is there anything further than that?

K: Oh yes, there is. There is a great deal more. Is listening to a sound within an area? Or am I listening to what you are saying without the verbal sound? If there is a verbal sound, I am not listening, I am understanding only the words. But you want to convey to me something much more than the words. So if the words are making a sound in my hearing, I can't deeply understand the depth of what you are saying. So I want to find out something much more. We started with the present. The present is the now. The now is the whole movement of time-thought. It is the whole structure. If the structure of time and thought ends, the now has a totally different meaning. The now then is nothing. When we use the word *nothing*, zero contains all the figures. So nothing contains all. But we are afraid to be nothing.

PJ: When you say it contains the all, is it the essence of all human and racial and environmental factors, nature, and the cosmos, as such?

K: I am talking of the fact of a realization that there is nothing. The psyche is a bundle of memories, and those memories are dead. They operate, they function, but they are the outcome of past experience, which is gone. I am a movement of memories. Now, if I have an insight into that, I am nothing, there is nothing, I don't exist.

PJ: You talked about sound and listening.

K: Listening without sound. Do you see the beauty of it?

PJ: Yes. It is possible when the mind itself is totally still.

K: No, don't bring in the mind for the moment. When the brain is quiet, absolutely quiet, there is no sound made by the word. That is real listening. The word has given me what you want to convey. You want to tell me, 'I am going this afternoon.' I listen to that...

PJ: But the brain has not been active in listening.

K: Yes. And the brain, when active, is noise, is sound. This is very interesting. What is sound? Pure sound can exist only when there is space and silence; otherwise it is just noise.

I would like to come back to the question. All one's education, all one's past experience and knowledge is a movement in becoming, inwardly as well as outwardly. Becoming is the accumulation of memory—more and more and more memories—which is called knowledge. Now, as long as that movement exists, there is the fear of being nothing. But when one really sees the fallacy, the illusion of becoming something; sees that this becoming is time-thought and endless conflict, that very perception, that insight that there is nothing, is the ending of that. That is, the ending of the movement which is the psyche, which is time-thought—the ending of that is to be nothing. *Nothing* then contains the whole universe—not my petty little fears, petty little anxieties and problems, and my sorrow with regard to a dozen things. After all, *nothing* means the entire world of compassion. Compassion is nothing. And therefore that nothingness is supreme intelligence. That is all there is.

So why are human beings frightened of being nothing? I am really a verbal illusion, I am nothing but dead memories; that's a fact. I don't like to think I am nothing but memories. But the truth is that I am memories. If I have no memory I am in a state of amnesia. Or I understand the whole movement of memory, which is time-thought, and see the fact that as long as there is this movement there must be endless conflict, struggle, pain. And when there is an insight into that, *nothing* means something entirely different. That nothing *is* the present. It is not a varying present, it isn't one day this and the next day something else. Being nothing means no time; therefore it is not ending one day and beginning another day.

Brockwood 1979: Conversation with Pupul Jayakar #2
Fire in the Mind, pp. 260-63

David Bohm: Are we saying that insight is an energy which illuminates the activity of the brain? And that in this illumination, the brain itself begins to act differently.

Krishnamurti: You are quite right. That's all. That is what takes place. Yes.

DB: We say the source of this illumination is not in the material process; it has no cause.

K: No cause.

DB: But it is a real energy.

K: It is pure energy. Is there action without cause?

DB: Yes, without time. Cause implies time.

K: That is, this flash has altered completely the pattern which the material process has set.

DB: Could you say that the material process generally operates in a kind of darkness, and therefore it has set itself on a wrong path?

K: In darkness, yes. That is clear. The material process acts in ignorance, in darkness. And this flash of insight enlightens the whole field, which means that ignorance and darkness have been dispelled. I will hold to that.

DB: You could say, then, that darkness and light cannot coexist for obvious reasons. Nevertheless the very existence of light is to change the process of darkness.

K: Quite right.

Questioner: But what contributes the flash?

K: We haven't come to that yet. I want to go step by step into this. What has happened is that the material process has worked in darkness and has brought about confusion and all the mess that exists in the world. But this flash of insight wipes away the darkness. Which means that the material process is not then working in darkness.

DB: Right. But now let's make another point clear. When the flash has gone, the light continues.

K: The light is there; the flash is the light.

DB: At a certain moment the flash is immediate, but then, as you work from there, there is still light.

K: Why do you differentiate flash from light?

DB: Simply because the word "flash" suggests something that happens in one moment.

K: Yes.

DB: You see, we are saying that insight would only last in that moment.

K: We must go slowly.

DB: Well, it is a matter of language.

K: Is it merely a matter of language?

DB: Perhaps not, but if you use the word "flash," there is the analogy of lightning, giving light for a moment, but then the next moment you are in darkness, until there is a further flash of lightning.

K: It is not like that.

DB: So what is it? Is it that the light suddenly turns on and stays on?

K: No. Because when we say "stays on" or "goes off," we are thinking in terms of time.

DB: We have to clear this up, because it is the question everybody will put.

K: The material process is working in darkness, in time, in knowledge, in ignorance, and so on. When insight takes place, there is the dispelling of that darkness. That is all we are saying. Insight dispels that darkness. And thought, which is the material process, no longer works in darkness. Therefore that light has altered—no, it has ended—ignorance.

DB: So we say that this darkness is really something which is built into the content of thought.

K: The content is darkness.

DB: That's right. Then that light has dispelled that ignorance.

K: That's right. Dispelled the content.

DB: But still we have to be very careful, since we still have content in the usually accepted sense of the word; we know all kinds of things.

K: Of course.

DB: So we can't say that the light has dispelled *all* the content.

K: It has dispelled the centre of darkness.

DB: Yes, the source, the creator of darkness.

K: Which is the self, right? It has dispelled the centre of darkness, which is the self.

DB: We could say that the self, which is part of the content—that part of the content which is the centre of darkness, which creates it and maintains it—is dispelled.

K: Yes, I hold to that.

DB: We see now that this means a physical change in the brain cells. That centre, that content which is the centre, is a certain set, form, disposition, of all the brain cells, and it in some way alters.

K: Obviously! You see, this has enormous significance, in our relationship with our society, in everything. Now, the next question is how does this flash come about? Let's begin the other way round. How does love come about? How does peace come about? Peace is causeless; violence has cause. How does that causeless thing come about when my whole life is causation? No, there is no "how," right? The "how" implies a cause, so there is no "how."

Q: Are you saying that since it is without cause, it is something that just exists?

K: No, I don't say that it exists. That is a dangerous statement.

Q: It has to exist at some point.

K: No. The moment you say it exists, it is not.

DB: You see, the danger is that it is part of the content.

K: The question you put was about a mutation in the brain calls. That question has been put after a series of discussions. And we have come to a point when we say that the flash, that light, has no cause; that the light operates on that which has cause, which is the darkness. That darkness exists as long as the self is there; it is the originator of that darkness, but light dispels the very centre of darkness. That's all. We have come to that point. And therefore there is a mutation. Then I say that the question of how do I get this flash of insight, how does it happen, is a wrong question. There is no "how."

Q: There is no "how," but there is darkness and there is light.

K: Just see first there is no "how." If you show me how, you are back into the darkness. Right?

DB: Yes.

K: It is a tremendous thing to understand that. I am asking something else, which is why is it that we have no insight at all? Why is it that this insight doesn't start from our childhood?

Ojai 1980: Conversation with David Bohm #6
The Ending of Time, pp. 161-65

INQUIRY AND INVESTIGATION

To explore there must be freedom. To explore really deeply, lastingly, you must leave your books, your ideas, your traditions, because without freedom no exploration is possible. No inquiry is ever possible when the mind is tethered to any kind of dogma, to a tradition, to a belief and so on. The difficulty with most of us is not that we are not capable of inquiring, not that we are incapable of investigating, but we are apparently totally incapable of letting things go, putting things aside, and therefore with a fresh mind, with a young mind, with an innocent mind, looking at the world and all the appalling things that are taking place in it. . . .

There are two ways of questioning. One is to question with a motive and therefore try to find an answer to the question; the other is to question without a motive and therefore seeking no answer. It is really important . . . to understand the difference between these two questionings.

Most of us do question, and our questioning is a reaction. I do not like something, and I question and reject it or modify it; my questioning is according to the urge or the demand of what I want. So, that kind of questioning has a motive behind it, and that questioning is a reaction. We know what a reaction is: I do not like something and I revolt against it. That revolt is merely a reaction, a response to something which I do not like. But there is a different questioning which is without a motive, which is not a reaction—which is to observe, to question the thing which is a fact. . . .

There are two ways of listening. One way is, you merely hear the words and pursue the meaning of words—which is to listen, to hear comparatively, which is to compare, which is to condemn, translate, interpret what is being said. That is what most people do; that is how we listen. When something is said, your brain immediately translates it as a reaction into your own terminology, into your own experiences, and you either accept what pleases or reject what does not please. You are merely reacting, you don't listen.

And then there is the other way of listening. That requires immense attention because in that listening there is no translation, there is no interpretation, no condemning, no comparison: you are just listening with all your being. A mind that is capable of so attentively listening understands immediately; it is free of time and of the brain which is the result of the social structure in which we have been brought up. As long as that brain has not become completely still—but is intensely alive, active—every thought, every experience is translated by that brain according to its conditioning, and therefore every thought, every feeling prevents total inquiry, total investigation. . . .

The brain must be aware of itself, and therefore it must question itself without seeking an answer because every answer will be projected from its own past, and therefore when you question seeking an answer, the answer is still within the boundaries of the conditioned mind . . . When you question— that is, when you are aware of yourself, of your activities, of your ways of thinking, feeling, of the way you talk, of the way you move, of everything else—don't seek an answer, but look at it, observe it. Then out of that observation, you will see that the brain begins to lose its conditioned state. . . .

So inquiry, investigation, is into yourself first and foremost, not into what Shankara, Buddha, or your guru has told you, but inquiry into yourself, into the ways of your mind, of your brain, into the ways of your thought.

Bombay 1962: Talk #1
CW Vol. XIII, pp. 113, 115, 117 & 118

What is that thing which, being understood, being explored, having its significance fully grasped, will help us to unravel and resolve the detail? Surely it is the mind, is it not? When I use that word *mind,* obviously you must have a reaction to that word, and that reaction depends upon your reading, your environmental influences, how much or how little you have thought about it, and so on. So, what is the mind? If I can understand the workings of that extraordinary thing called the mind—the totality of it, the feeling, the nature, the amazing capacity of it; its profundity, width and quality—then whatever its reaction, which is merely the product of its culture, environment, education, reading and so on, I can tackle it. So, we are going to . . . explore this thing called the mind. But obviously you cannot explore it if you already have an idea about it. If you say, 'The mind is *atman,*' it is finished; you have stopped all exploration, investigation, inquiry. Or if you are a communist and say that the mind is merely the result of some influence, then also you are incapable of examining. It is very important to understand that if you approach a problem with a mind already made up, you have stopped investigating the problem and therefore prevented the understanding of the problem. The socialist, the capitalist, the communist, who approaches the problem of starvation, does so with a system, a theory, and so what happens? He is incapable of making a further examination of the problem. Life does not stop, it is a movement, and if you approach it with a static mind you cannot touch it. Again, this is fairly clear. . . .

When I use the word *mind* I look at it without any conclusion; therefore I am capable of examining it, or rather the mind having no conclusion about itself is capable of looking at itself. A mind that starts to think from a conclusion is not really thinking. It is asking an enormous thing, is it not, for the mind to examine a problem without any conclusion. I do not know if you see this, that with most of us, thinking starts from a conclusion: that there is God or no God, reincarnation or no reincarnation, that the communist or the capitalist system will save the world. We start from one conclusion and go to another, and this process of moving from conclusion to conclusion we call thinking. And if you observe it, it is not thinking at all. Thinking implies a constant moving, a constant examination, a constant awareness of the movement of thought—not a fixed point from which to go to another fixed point.

So, we are going to find out what this extraordinary thing called the mind is, because that is the problem and nothing else. It is the mind that creates the problem; it is . . . thought, the conditioned mind . . . that is petty, narrow, bigoted, which has created beliefs, ideas, and knowledge, and which is crippled by its own concepts, vanities, greed, ambitions, and frustrations. So it is the mind which has to be understood, and that mind is the "me", that mind is the self—not some higher self. The mind invents the higher self and then says it is only a tool for the higher. Such thinking is absurd, immature; it is the mind which invents all these avenues of escape and then proceeds from there to assert. . . .

Can you experience directly the quality of this amazingly complex mind, the vastness of it, the immensity of it? . . . To understand the quality of the mind and its immensity, there must be freedom—freedom from all conditioning, from all conclusions—because it is only such a mind that is a young mind. And it is only the young mind that can move freely, investigate, be innocent.

Madras 1958: Talk #2
CW Vol. XI, pp. 63-64, 65 & 66

INVESTIGATION WITH SCHOOL STUDENTS

I t is very important while we are at . . . school to look at the rivers, the green fields and the trees; to have good food, but not food that is too tasty, that is too hot; not to eat too much; to enjoy games without competition; not to try to win for the college but to play for the sake of the game. From there you will find, if you are really observing, that the mind becomes very alert, watchful, recollected; and so, as you grow you are bound to enjoy things right through life. But merely to remain at the superficial level of enjoyment, and not to know the real depth of human capacity, is like living in a dirty street and trying to keep it clean. It always gets dirty, it will always be spoilt, it will always be corrupt. But if one can through the right kind of education know how to think and to go beyond all thought, then in that there is extraordinary peace, a bliss which the superficial mind, living in its own superficial happiness, can never find.

You have heard what I said about food, clothes and cleanliness. Try to find out for yourself something more beyond it. . . . After all, it is only when you are young that you can be revolutionaries, not when you are 60 or 70. Perhaps a few of us may be, but the vast majority are not revolutionaries. As you grow older, you crystallize. It is only when you are young that there is the possibility of revolution, of revolt, of discontent. To have that revolt, there must be discontent all through life. There is nothing wrong with revolt. What is wrong is to find an avenue which will satisfy you, which will quiet the discontent. . . .

In the same way, to see below the surface of the mind, to know the ripples in it and all its activities, you must be capable of going deep down into the mind. It is important to know that the mind is not just the little layer of superficial activity, that you are not merely studying to pass examinations, not merely following some tradition in the matter of what you wear, doing *puja* or something else. To go below the superficial activities, you must have a mind that can understand how to go deep. I think that is one of the functions of education—not to be merely satisfied with the surface, whether it is beautiful or ugly, but to be able to go deep like the diver in his diving suit, so that in the depths you can freely breathe, so that you can find out in those depths all the intricacies of life, the limitations, the fluctuations, the varieties of thought—because in oneself, one is all that—and then go beyond all that, transcend it.

You cannot go very deep if you do not know the surface of your mind. To know the surface, one has to watch; the mind has to watch the way one dresses, puts on a sacred thread, does *puja*, and understand why. Then you can go deep. But to go deep, you must have a very simple mind. That is why a mind that is held in conclusions, in condemnation, in comparison, can never go beyond its own superficial activities.

Rajghat 1954: Talk to Students #12
CW Vol. VIII, pp. 119-20 & 122

COMPARISON AND COMPETITION

Most people think that learning is encouraged through comparison, whereas the contrary is the fact. Comparison brings about frustration and merely encourages envy, which is called competition. Like other forms of persuasion, comparison prevents learning and breeds fear. Ambition also breeds fear. Ambition, whether personal or identified with the collective, is always antisocial. So-called noble ambition in relationship is fundamentally destructive.

We are concerned with the total development of each human being, helping him to realize his own highest and fullest capacity—not some fictitious capacity which the educator has in view as a concept or an ideal. Any spirit of comparison prevents this full flowering of the individual, whether he is to be a scientist or a gardener. The fullest capacity of the gardener is the same as the fullest capacity of the scientist when there is no comparison; but when comparison comes in, then there is the disparagement and the envious reactions which create conflict between man and man. Like sorrow, love is not comparative; it cannot be compared with the greater or the lesser.

Sorrow is sorrow, as love is love, whether it be in the rich or in the poor.

The fullest development of every individual creates a society of equals. The present social struggle to bring about equality on the economic or some spiritual level has no meaning at all. Social reforms aimed at establishing equality breed other forms of antisocial activity, but with right education there is no need to seek equality through social and other reforms because envy with its comparison of capacities ceases.

We must differentiate here between function and status. Status, with all its emotional and hierarchical prestige, arises only through the comparison of functions as the high and the low. When each individual is flowering to his fullest capacity, there is then no comparison of functions; there is only the expression of capacity as a teacher, or a prime minister, or a gardener, and so status loses its sting of envy.

Functional or technical capacity is now recognized through having a degree after one's name, but if we are truly concerned with the total development of the human being our approach is entirely different. An individual who has the capacity may take a degree or he may not, as he pleases. But he will know for himself his own deep capabilities, which will not be framed by a degree, and their expression will not bring about that self-centred confidence which mere technical capacity usually breeds. Such confidence is comparative and therefore antisocial. Comparison may exist for utilitarian purposes, but it is not for the educator to compare the capacities of his students and give greater or lesser evaluation.

Intelligence is the capacity to deal with life as a whole, and giving grades or marks to the student does not assure intelligence; on the contrary, it degrades human dignity. This comparative evaluation cripples the mind—which does not mean that the teacher must not observe the progress of every student and keep a record of it. Parents, naturally anxious to know the progress of their children, will want a report; but if, unfortunately, they do not understand what the educator is trying to do, the report will become an instrument of coercion to produce the results they desire, and so undo the work of the educator.

From the Introduction to Life Ahead

Almost all human beings in their lives desire power and wealth. When there is wealth there is a sense of freedom, and pleasure is pursued. The desire for power seems be an instinct which expresses itself in many ways. It is in the priest, the guru, the husband or the wife, or in one boy over another. This desire to dominate or to submit is one of the conditions of man, probably inherited from the animal. This aggressiveness and the yielding to it pervert all relationships throughout life. This has been the pattern from the beginning of time. Man has accepted this as a natural way of life, with all the conflicts and miseries it brings.

Basically, measurement is involved in it—the more and the less, the greater and the smaller—which is essentially comparison. One is always comparing oneself with another, comparing one painting with another; there is comparison between the greater power and the lesser, between the timid and the aggressive. It begins almost at birth and continues throughout life—this constant measurement of power, position, wealth. This is encouraged in schools, colleges and universities. Their whole system of gradation is this comparative value of knowledge. When A is compared to B who is clever, bright, assertive, that very comparison destroys A. This destruction takes the form of competition, of imitation, and conformity to the patterns set by B. This breeds, consciously or unconsciously, antagonism, jealousy, anxiety, and even fear; and this becomes the condition in which A lives for the rest of his life, always measuring, always comparing psychologically and physically.

This comparison is one of the many aspects of violence. The word *more* is always comparative, as is the word *better*. The question is, can the educator put aside all comparison, all measurement, in his teaching? Can he take the student as he is, not as what he should be, not make judgements based on comparative evaluations? It is only when there is comparison between the one called clever and the one called dull that there is such a quality as dullness.

The Whole Movement of Life is Learning, pp. 101-02

We are always comparing what we are with what we should be. The *should be* is a projection of what we think ought to be. We compare ourselves with our neighbour, with the riches he has which we haven't. We compare ourselves with those who are more bright, more intellectual, more affectionate, more kind, more famous, more this and that. The *more* plays an extraordinarily important part in our lives, and the measuring that takes place in each one of us; measuring ourselves with something is one of the primary causes of conflict. In this is involved competition, comparison with this and with that, and we are caught in this conflict. Why is there comparison at all? Put this question to yourself. Why do you compare yourself with another? Of course, one of the tricks of commercial propaganda is to make you think you are not what you should be and all the rest of it. And from a very young age it begins, you must be as clever as another, through examinations and so on. Why do we compare ourselves at all, psychologically? Please find out. If I don't compare, what am I? I may be dull, empty, stupid—I'll be what I am. If I don't compare myself with another I shall be what I am. But through comparison I hope to evolve, grow, become more intelligent, more beautiful, more this and more that. Will I? The fact is that I am what I am, and by comparing I am fragmenting that fact, the actuality, and that is a waste of energy; whereas not to compare but to be what actually I am, is to have the tremendous energy to look. When you can look without comparison you're beyond all comparison. Which doesn't imply a mind that is stagnant with contentment, on the contrary. . . .

Can I really look at myself as I am without any comparison, condemnation and judgement? When I can, I am already out of society because society always thinks in terms of the great and the small, the powerful and the weak, the beautiful and the ugly. With one act I've understood this whole process of fragmentation, and therefore I do not belong to any church, any group, any religion, any nationality, to any party.

Talks & Dialogues Saanen 1967, p. 23

Questioner: How can one be satisfied with what one is?

Krishnamurti: Dissatisfaction comes when there is comparison. When you see somebody else having more and you having less, and you compare yourself with that somebody, then dissatisfaction comes; but if you do not compare, then there is no problem. But not to compare requires a great deal of interest and understanding because all our education, all our training, is based on comparison: 'That boy is not as good as you,' 'you are not as clever as that boy,' and so on. Then you struggle, and this boy struggles like you. So we keep this game of constant comparison and struggle. But if you love the thing which you are doing, you do it because you love it and not because somebody else is doing it better than you or you are doing it better than somebody else. When you have no comparison of any kind, then the thing that you are doing, that itself begins to produce its own depths, its own heights.

Rajghat Varanasi1954: Talk to Students #14, CW Vol. VIII, p. 134

HARMONY OF BODY, MIND AND HEART

I want to find out what is harmony between the mind, the body and the heart, a total sense of being whole without fragmentation, without the overdevelopment of the intellect, but with the intellect operating clearly, objectively, sanely; and the heart not operating with sentiment, emotionalism, outbreaks of hysteria, but with a quality of affection, care, love, compassion, vitality; and the body with its own intelligence, not interfered with by the intellect. The feeling that everything is operating, functioning, beautifully like a marvellous machine is important. Is this possible?

Exploration into Insight, p.52

We live by our senses. One of them is usually dominant: the listening, the seeing, the tasting seem to be separate from each other; but is this a fact? Or is it that we have given to one or other a greater importance, or rather that thought has given the greater importance? One may hear great music and delight in it, and yet be insensitive to other things. One may have a sensitive taste and be wholly insensitive to delicate colour. This is fragmentation. When each fragment is aware only of itself, then fragmentation is maintained. In this way energy is broken up. If this is so, as it appears to be, is there a non-fragmentary awareness by all the senses?

Thought is part of the senses. Can the body be aware of itself? Not you being aware of your own body, but the body itself being aware. This is very important to find out. It cannot be taught by another, for then it is second-hand information which thought is imposing upon itself. You must discover for yourself whether the whole organism, the physical entity, can be aware of itself. You may be aware of the movement of an arm, a leg or the head, and through that movement sense that you are becoming aware of the whole, but what we are asking is: can the body be aware of itself without any movement? This is essential to find out, because thought has imposed its pattern on the body, what it thinks is right exercise, right food, and so on. So there is the domination of thought over the organism; there is consciously or unconsciously a struggle between thought and the organism. In this way thought is destroying the natural intelligence of the body itself.

Does the body, the physical organism, have its own intelligence? It has when all the senses are acting together in harmony so that there is no straining, no emotional or sensory demands of desire. When one is hungry one eats, but usually taste, formed by habit, dictates what one eats. So fragmentation takes place. A healthy body can be brought about only through the harmony of all the senses, which is the intelligence of the body itself. What we are asking is: doesn't disharmony bring about the wastage of energy? Can the organism's own intelligence, which has been suppressed or destroyed by thought, be awakened?

The Whole Movement of Life is Learning, pp. 80-82

THINKING TOGETHER

It is important that we, you and the speaker, think together. By *thinking together* we mean not merely accepting any kind of opinion or evaluation but observing together, not only externally what is happening in the world but also what is happening to all of us inwardly, psychologically. Externally, outwardly, there is great uncertainty, confusion, wars, or the threat of war. There are wars going on now in some parts of the world; human beings are killing each other. That is not happening in the West, but there is the threat of nuclear war, and the preparation for war. And we ordinary human beings do not seem to be able to do anything about it. There are demonstrations, hunger strikes, terrorism, and so on; there is one tribal group against another. The scientists are contributing to that, and the philosophers, though they may talk against it, are inwardly continuing to think in terms of nationalism, according to their own particular careers. So, that is what is actually going on in the outward world, which any intelligent human being can observe.

And inwardly, in our own minds and in our own hearts, we ourselves are also very confused. There is no security, not only for ourselves but for the future generation. Religions have divided human beings as the Christians, the Hindus, the Muslims, and the Buddhists. So considering all this, observing objectively, calmly, without any prejudice, it is naturally important that together we think about it all. *Think together*—not having opinions opposing other sets of opinions, not having one conclusion against another conclusion, one ideal against another ideal, but rather thinking together and seeing what we human beings can do. The crisis is not in the economic world, nor in the political world: the crisis is in consciousness. I think very few of us realize this. The crisis is in our mind and in our heart, that is, the crisis is in our consciousness. Our consciousness is our whole existence—our beliefs, with our conclusions, with our nationalism; with all the fears that we have, the pleasures, the apparently insoluble problem of sorrow; the thing that we call love, compassion; and the problem of death, if there is anything hereafter; and the question of meditation, if there is something eternal, beyond time, beyond thought—that is the content of our consciousness, that is the content of every human being, in whatever part of the world he lives. The content of our consciousness is the common ground of all humanity.

The Network of Thought, pp. 84-85

I hope we can think together. . . . If one person has a particular point of view and another sticks to his opinion, then it's impossible to think together. If you are prejudiced and the speaker has a particular point of view, then we cannot possibly think together. Thinking together does not mean agreeing, but rather together as two human beings—not Americans, Hindus, and all that business—two human beings who are confronted with the problem that we have created this society which is so terrifying. And as human beings we have to radically change ourselves. Is that possible? Is it possible for the human mind which has evolved through time, millennia upon millennia, passing through a great many experiences, sufferings, many conflicting incidents, wars—the mind of the human being, this brain, which is not yours or mine but which has evolved for five or ten million years? It's the human brain, not a particular brain; we have reduced it to a particular brain, "mine" and "yours", but if you examine it very carefully you will find this brain, which has evolved through time, is the brain of mankind. . . . And this brain has functioned in various patterns—the pattern of fear, the pattern of pleasure, the pattern of reward and punishment—through all the millennia it has developed these patterns. Is it possible to bring about not another series of pleasurable patterns, or patterns of fear, belief, and so on, but to go beyond all these patterns? Otherwise there is no radical change, there is no psychological revolution. . . . We are together thinking, inquiring into the problem. . . . We are inquiring, talking together, as two friends.

Ojai 1980: Talk #3, 10ᵗʰ May

THINKING TOGETHER ABOUT
EDUCATION

Questioner: What are your ideas about education?

Krishnamurti: I think mere ideas are no good at all because one idea is as good as another, depending on whether the mind accepts or rejects it; but perhaps it would be worthwhile to find out what we mean by education. Let us see if we can think out together the whole significance of education, and not merely think in terms of my idea or your idea, or the idea of some specialist.

Why do we educate our children at all? Is it to help the child to understand the whole significance of life, or merely to prepare him to earn a livelihood in a particular culture or society? Which is it that we want? Not what we should want, or what is desirable, but what is it that we as parents actually insist on? We want the child to conform, to be a respectable citizen in a corrupt society, a society that is at war both within itself and with other societies, that is brutal, acquisitive, violent, greedy, with occasional spots of affection, tolerance and kindliness. That is what we actually want, is it not? If the child does not fit into society—whether it be communist, socialist or capitalist—we are afraid of what will happen to him; so we begin to educate him to conform to the pattern of our own making. That is all we want where the child is concerned, and that is essentially what is taking place. And any revolt of the child against society, against the pattern of conformity, we call delinquency. We want the children to conform; we want to control their minds, to shape their conduct, their way of living, so that they will fit into the pattern of society. That is what every parent wants, is it not? And that is exactly what is happening, whether it be in America or in Europe, in Russia or in India. The pattern may vary slightly, but they all want the child to conform.

Now, is that education? Or does education mean that the parents and the teachers themselves see the significance of the whole pattern and are helping the child from the very beginning to be alert to all its influences? Seeing the full significance of the pattern with its religious, social, and economic influences, its influences of class, of family, of tradition; seeing the significance of all this for oneself and helping the child to understand and not be caught in it, that may be education. To educate the child may be to help him to be outside of society, so that he creates his own society. Since our society is not at all what it should be, why encourage the child to stay within its pattern? At present, we force the child to conform to a social pattern which we have established individually, as a family and as the collective; and he unfortunately inherits not only our property but some of our psychological characteristics as well. So from the very beginning he is a slave to the environment.

Seeing all this, if we really love our children and are therefore deeply concerned about education, we will contrive from the very beginning to bring about an atmosphere which will encourage them to be free. A few real educators have thought about all this, but unfortunately very few parents ever think about it at all. We leave it to the experts—religion to the priest, psychology to the psychologist, and our children to the so-called teachers. The parent is also the educator; he is the teacher and also the one who learns—not only the child.

This is a very complex problem and if we really wish to resolve it we must go into it most profoundly; and then we shall find out how to bring about the right kind of education.

Brussels 1956: Talk #6, CW Vol. X, pp. 64-65

NEGATIVE THINKING

N egative thinking is the highest form of thinking. By *negative* I do not mean the opposite of the positive. Most of us think positively, in terms of *do* and *don't,* which is adjustment to a conclusion, to a pattern of thought or action. The pattern may be the result of a great deal of experience, it may be the outcome of research and many experiments, but it is still a pattern; and thinking according to a pattern, however conclusive or satisfactory, is a process of conformity which always conditions the mind.

But to deny such positive thinking and merely to revolt against the pattern will in no way create thinking which is of the highest quality. The highest form of thinking is negative thinking, that is, just to be aware of the fallacies of positive thinking, to see the conflicts it creates, and from there to think clearly, dispassionately, without any prejudice or conclusion.

New Delhi 1960: Talk #1, CW Vol. XI, p. 329

One begins to discover what is the true religious spirit only through negative thinking, because negative thinking is the highest form of thinking. I mean by negative thinking the discarding, the tearing through of false things, breaking down the things that man has put together for his own security, for his own inward safety—all the various defences and the mechanism of thought which builds these defences. I feel one must shatter them, go through them rapidly, swiftly, and see if there is anything beyond. To tear through all these false things is not a reaction to what exists. To find out what is the religious spirit and to approach it negatively, one must see what one believes, why one believes, why one accepts all the innumerable conditionings which organized religions throughout the world impose on the human mind. Why do you believe in God? Why do you not believe in God? Why do you have so many dogmas, beliefs?

You may say that if one goes through all these so-called positive structures behind which the mind takes shelter, goes through them without trying to find something more, then there will be nothing left, only despair. But I think one has to go through despair also. Despair exists only when there is hope—the hope of being secure, being permanently comfortable, perpetually mediocre, perpetually happy. For most of us, despair is the reaction to hope. But to discover what the religious spirit is, it seems to me that inquiry must come into being without any provocation, without any reaction. If your search is only a reaction—because you want to find more inward security—then your search is merely for greater comfort, whether in a belief, in an idea, or in knowledge, experience. Such thought, born of reaction, can only produce further reactions, and therefore there is no liberation from the process of reaction which prevents discovery.

There must be a negative approach, which means that the mind must become aware of the conditioning imposed by society with regard to morality, aware of the innumerable sanctions which religion imposes, and aware also of how in rejecting these outward impositions one has cultivated certain inward resistances, the conscious and unconscious beliefs which are based on experience, knowledge, and which become the guiding factors. The mind which would discover what the true religious spirit is must be in a state of revolution, which means the destruction of all the false things which have been imposed on it, either by the outward pressures or by itself; for the mind is always seeking security. So it seems to me that the religious spirit has within it this constant state of a mind which never builds, never constructs for its own safety. Because if the mind builds with the urge to be secure, then it lives behind its own walls and so is not capable of discovering if there is something new.

So death, the destruction of the old, is necessary—the destruction of tradition, the total freedom from what has been, the removal of the things that it has accumulated as memory through the centuries of many yesterdays. Then you might say, 'What remains? All that I am is this story, this history, the experiences; if all that is gone, wiped away, what remains?' First of all, is it possible to wipe all that away? We may talk about it, but is it actually possible? I say it *is* possible. Not by influence, not by coercion—that is too silly, too immature—but I say that it can be done if one goes into it very deeply, brushing aside all authority. That state of wiping the slate clean—which means dying every day, and from moment to moment, to the things one has accumulated—requires a great deal of energy and deep insight. And that is part of the religious spirit.

London 1961: Talk #11, CW Vol. XII, pp. 170-71

INTELLIGENCE

David Bohm: About *intelligence,* I always like to look up the origin of a word as well as its meaning. It is very interesting; it comes from *inter* and *legere* which means 'to read between'. So, it seems to me that you could say that thought is like the information in a book and that intelligence has to read it, the meaning of it. I think this gives a rather good notion of intelligence.

Krishnamurti: To read between the lines.

DB: Yes, to see what it means. There is also another relevant meaning given in the dictionary, which is, *mental alertness.*

K: Yes, mental alertness.

DB: This is very different from what people have in mind when they measure intelligence. Now, considering many of the things you have said, you would say intelligence is not thought. You say thought takes place in the old brain, it is a physical process, electrochemical; it has been amply proved by science that all thought is essentially a physical, chemical process.

Then we could say, perhaps, that intelligence is not of the same order, it is not of the order of time at all. . . . Intelligence "reads between the lines" of thought, sees the meaning of it. There is one more point before we start on this question: if you say thought is physical, then the mind or intelligence or whatever you want to call it, seems different, it is of a different order. Would you say there is a real difference between the physical and intelligence?

K: Are we saying that thought is matter? Let us put it differently.

DB: I would rather call it a *material process.*

K: All right, thought is a material process; and what is the relationship between that and intelligence? Is intelligence the product of thought?

DB: I think we can take for granted that it is not.

K: Why do we take it for granted?

DB: Simply because thought is mechanical.

K: Thought is mechanical—that is right.

DB: Intelligence is not.

K: So, thought is measurable, intelligence is not. And how does it happen that this intelligence comes into existence? If thought has no relationship with intelligence, then is the cessation of thought the awakening of intelligence? Or is it that intelligence, being independent of thought, not of time, therefore exists always?

DB: That raises many difficult questions.

K: I know.

The Awakening of Intelligence, pp. 509-11

Our minds are the result of thousands of experiences, and man has been searching for this eternity—not immortality; immortality is merely the continuity of one's own ignorance. . . . There is this deep-rooted, deep-laden seed which man has not cultivated, nourished, looked after, cared for, which is the beginning of that which he has sought. We have cultivated every other faculty; if you observe within yourself, we have cultivated through time the idea of the individual, the "you" and the "me", "we" and "they". This has been handed down from generation to generation. Is that so? Is it a reality or a fiction, something thought has carefully cultivated? Please . . . do not resist. I know you all believe in individuality—your fulfilment, your immortality, your birth after this and after that—you are rooted in this individual concept. Now we are asking if that is so. We have also cultivated various other things. By questioning everything that we hold both consciously as well as unconsciously, in questioning objectively, sanely, rationally; not wanting to change it but seeing things as they are, what actually *is*; not moving away from it or escaping from it, not wanting to go beyond it—and that calls for scrupulous attention—there comes intelligence. The etymological meaning of that word *intelligence* is to be able to understand, to be able to discern, to be able to see without direction, without pressure what actually is going on. In the pure perception of what is going on, there is insight into what is going on; and that insight is the movement of intelligence—not cleverness, not erudition, not experience, but the immediate perception of what is true. The perception of what is true can only take place if there is no direction, no motivation, just the pure, unadulterated, unpremeditated observation. That intelligence wipes away the centre, the "me" from which we are acting.

Madras 1979: Talk #2, 23rd December

We have seen that thought itself is limited. . . . And whatever thought has done or is doing—killing animals, whales, dolphins, baby seals, worshiping in a marvellous cathedral—must create disorder. Do you see that, not as an idea but actually? Thought has created nationalities—American, English, German, French, and linguistically driven each one in a different direction. So thought has created . . . disorder.

If thought has created disorder, what will bring about order? Man says that we cannot do anything about this disorder, but God will bring order—the guru, the priest, somebody—an external agency will bring about order, therefore let us pray, let us attend churches. It is all the movement of thought. And thought, whatever it does, is disorder. If one realizes that, sees that . . . the perception of that is intelligence. . . . The perception that thought, whatever it does, has created and is creating disorder, that very perception is insight, which is intelligence. And that insight brings order.

Ojai 1978: Talk #2, 2nd April

INTELLIGENCE, GLOBAL THINKING
AND EDUCATION

It is important that we think of this whole thing totally anew and not do patchwork reform here and there. Shouldn't we try to solve our problems not in terms of America or Russia or any other particular country, but as a whole? Shouldn't we approach this problem of man's existence not as Americans or Englishmen, but in terms of human relationship? Until we do that we shall have constant wars, there will be starvation in the world. There *is* starvation, perhaps not in America, but in Asia, and until that problem is solved there will be no peace here. You cannot solve it as an American or a Russian, as a communist or a capitalist: you can solve it only as a human being. . . .

If you really understand this as a simple individual, then you will be solving the problem. But if you are merely concerned with trying to help your son to fulfil himself in a particular society, if you are merely concerned with a particular problem—which of course must be dealt with, but which cannot be dealt with unless you tackle the problem as a whole—then you will find no answer and therefore you will have more complications, more misery.

So, we have to fundamentally tackle the problem of what education is. Is it merely to teach a technique so that the young person will have a job? Or is it to create an atmosphere of true freedom?—not to do what one likes, but freedom to cultivate that intelligence which will meet every experience, every conditioning influence, meet it, understand it, and go beyond it. That requires a great deal of perception, a great deal of insight and intelligence on the part of each one of us. But we are all so frightened because we want to be secure. The moment we seek security, the shadow of fear is cast, and in trying to overcome that fear we further condition ourselves, we condition our minds and create a society which is bound to limit our thinking. And the more efficient a society becomes, the more conditioned it is.

New York 1954: Talk #3, CW Vol. VIII, pp. 226-27

INTELLIGENCE AND CLEVERNESS

Questioner: Is there any difference between cleverness and intelligence?

Krishnamurti: Don't you think that there is a vast difference? You might be very clever in your subject, be able to pass exams, argue out, argue with another student. You might be afraid—afraid of what your father may say, what your neighbour, your sister or somebody else says. You may be very clever and yet have fear; and if you have fear, you have no intelligence. Your cleverness is not really intelligence. Most of us who are in schools become more and more clever and cunning as we grow older because that is what we are trained to do: to outdo somebody else in business or in the black market, to be so ambitious that we get ahead of others, push others aside. But intelligence is something quite different: it is a state in which your whole being, your whole mind and your emotions are integrated, are one. This integrated human being is an intelligent human being, not a clever person.

Rajghat Varanasi 1954: Talk to Students #4
CW Vol. VIII, p. 75

THE SCIENTIFIC MIND AND THE
RELIGIOUS MIND

A religious mind is free of the past, a religious mind is free of time, because time belongs to the positive and negative reactions. So, a religious mind is a mind that is capable of thinking precisely, not in terms of negative and positive; therefore such a religious mind has the scientific mind within it, but the scientific mind has not the religious mind within it. The religious mind contains the scientific mind, but the scientific mind cannot contain the religious mind because that is based on time, on knowledge, on achievement, success, utilization.

The religious mind is a mind that is capable of thinking precisely, clearly, sharply, which is the scientific mind. And it is the religious mind that is creative, not the scientific mind. The scientific mind can invent. Invention, capacity, gift, has nothing to do with creative being; writing a poem, painting pictures, composing music, is not the creative thing of the religious mind. So, the religious mind is the only mind that can respond totally to the present challenge and to all challenges at all times.

Bombay 1961: Talk #5, CW Vol. XII, p. 80

The really scientific mind and the really religious mind are the only two minds that can exist in the twentieth century—not the superstitious, believing, temple-going, church-worshiping mind. The scientific mind is the mind that pursues fact. To pursue materialistic fact, which is to discover under the microscope, needs immense accumulated knowledge. And such a scientific mind is the product of the twentieth century. So, one begins to see that a scientific mind, the so-called educated mind, the mind that has learnt a certain technique and thinks rationally and with knowledge, always moves from the known to the known, from fact to fact. Such a mind is absolutely necessary because it can reason logically, sanely, rationally, precisely. But such a mind cannot, obviously, free itself to inquire into what is beyond the accumulated knowledge—which is the function of religion.

Madras 1961: Talk #8, CW Vol. XII, p. 322

A religious mind is free of all authority. It is extremely difficult to be free from authority—not only the authority imposed by another but also the authority of the experience which one has gathered, which is of the past, which is tradition. The religious mind has no beliefs, it has no dogmas; it moves from fact to fact. Therefore the religious mind is the scientific mind. But the scientific mind is not the religious mind. The religious mind includes the scientific mind, but the mind that is trained in the knowledge of science is not a religious mind.

Paris 1961: Talk #9, CW Vol. XII, p. 270

THE SCIENTIFIC MIND AND
THE RELIGIOUS MIND
(WITH SCHOOL STUDENTS)

I want to talk about something which concerns the whole world, about which the whole world is disturbed: it is the question of the religious spirit and the scientific mind. There are these two attitudes in the world. These are the only two attitudes in the world: the true religious spirit and the scientific mind. Every other activity is destructive, leading to a great deal of misery, confusion and sorrow.

The scientific mind is very factual. Discovery is its mission, its perception. It sees things through a microscope, through a telescope; everything is to be seen actually as it is. From that perception science draws conclusions, builds up theories. Such a mind moves from fact to fact. The spirit of science has nothing to do with individual conditions, with nationalism, with race, with prejudice. Scientists are there to explore matter, to investigate the structure of the earth and of the stars and the planets, to find out how to cure man's diseases, how to prolong man's life, to explain time, both the past and the future. But the scientific mind and its discoveries are used and exploited by the nationalistic mind, by the mind that is

India, by the mind that is Russia, by the mind that is America. Scientific discovery is utilized and exploited by sovereign states and continents.

Then there is the religious mind, the true religious mind, that does not belong to any cult, to any group, to any religion, to any organized church. The religious mind is not the Hindu mind, the Christian mind, the Buddhist mind, or the Muslim mind; the religious mind does not belong to any group which calls itself religious. The religious mind is not the mind that goes to churches, temples, mosques. Nor is it a religious mind that holds to certain forms of beliefs, dogmas. The religious mind is completely alone. It is a mind that has seen through the falsity of churches, dogmas, beliefs, traditions. Not being nationalistic, not being conditioned by its environment, such a mind has no horizons, no limits; it is explosive, new, young, fresh, innocent. The innocent mind, the young mind, the mind that is extraordinarily pliable, subtle, has no anchor. It is only such a mind that can experience that which you call God, that which is not measurable.

A human being is a true human being when the scientific spirit and the true religious spirit go together. . . . He is the true Brahmin, the new human being, who combines both the scientific and the religious mind, and therefore is harmonious without any contradiction within himself. The purpose of education is to create this new mind which is explosive and does not conform to a pattern which society has set.

Krishnamurti on Education, pp. 16-17

CREATIVE ENERGY

Krishnamurti: Has one got creative energy, and how can one release it? We have got plenty of energy when we want to do something. When we want to do something very badly, we have got enough energy to do it. When we want to play or go for a long walk, we have energy. When we want to hurt people, we have energy. When we get angry, that is an indication of energy. When we talk endlessly, that is also an expression of energy.

What is the difference between this and creative energy? . . . What is the difference between physical energy and energy that is brought about through friction, such as anger, tension, dislike. There is purely physical energy and there is the energy derived through tension, through conflict, through ambition. And is there any other kind of energy? We only know these two: the energy that a good, healthy body has—tremendous energy—and the energy that one gets through every kind of struggle, friction, conflict. Have you noticed this?—the great writers who lead terrible lives, miserable lives of conflict in their relationship with others and with people generally, this tension gives them a tremendous energy. And because they have got a certain capacity, a gift to write, that energy expresses itself through writing. . . .

Now, you see the two types: physical energy, and energy which comes through conflict and resistance, through fear or the pursuit of pleasure. Is there any other kind of energy? Is there energy which is without motive?

Beginnings of Learning, pp. 81-82

There is physical energy, and we have plenty of it because we have good food, rest and so on. Then there is psychological energy, which is dissipated in conflict. And I say that is a waste of energy.

So, can I act psychologically without wastage of energy, based on facts only and nothing else? Only facts and not psychological, emotional prejudice: 'I must, I must not.' Then you have harmony between the psyche and the physical; then you have a harmonious way of living. From there you can find out if there is another kind of energy of a totally different kind. But without having the harmony between the psyche and the physical, psychosomatic harmony, then your inquiry into the other has no meaning.

Now, what are you going to do with your life; what are you going to do this morning or this afternoon when this problem arises? It is going to arise every day of your life: come into the kitchen, go out for a walk, build an aeroplane, or go for a drive. . . . What you will do depends on how you have listened. If you have really listened you will, from now on, just act on facts—that's a marvellous thing, you don't know the beauty of it—just on facts, instead of bringing all your emotional circus into it.

Beginnings of Learning, pp. 92-93

THE CONSCIOUS AND THE
UNCONSCIOUS MIND

Culture can only produce religions, not a religious man. And . . . it is only the religious man who can really bring about a radical change within himself. Any change, any alteration within the conditioned mind of a particular culture is no real change, it is merely a continuation of the same thing, modified. I think this is fairly obvious if one thinks about it, that so long as I have the pattern of a Hindu, a Christian, a Buddhist, or what you will, any change I bring about within that pattern as a conscious change is still part of the pattern and therefore no change at all. Then the question arises: can I bring about a change through the unconscious? That is, either I start consciously to remove my prejudices, to change the pattern of my living, the way I think—which is a deliberate process in the pursuit of an ideal—or I try to bring about a change by delving into the unconscious.

In both these approaches is involved the problem of effort. I see I must change—for various reasons, from various motives—and I consciously set about changing. Then I realize, if I think about it at all, that it is not a real change, and so I delve into the unconscious, go into it very deeply, hoping through various forms of analysis to bring about a change, a modification or a deeper adjustment. Now I ask myself wheth-er this conscious and unconscious effort to change brings about a change at all. Or must one go beyond the conscious as well as the unconscious to bring about a radical change? Both the conscious desire as well as the unconscious urge to change imply effort. If you go into it very deeply you will see that in trying to change oneself into something else, there is always the one who makes the effort and that which is static, upon which the effort is exerted. So, in this process of desire to bring about a change, whether it is conscious or unconscious, there is always the thinker and the thought, the thinker try-ing to change his thought, the one who says, 'I must change,' and the state which he desires to change. So there is this dual-ity; and we are always, everlastingly, trying to bridge this gap through effort. I see in myself that there is, in the conscious as well as the unconscious, the maker of effort and that which he wishes to change. There is a division between that which I am and that which I wish to be, which means there is a division between the thinker and the thought, and so there is a con-flict. The thinker is always trying to overcome that conflict, consciously or unconsciously.

We are quite familiar with this process; it is what we are doing all the time. All our social structure, our morality, our adjustments and so on are based on it. But does that bring about a change? If not, then must there not be a change at a totally different level, which is not in the field either of the conscious or the unconscious? The whole field of the mind, the conscious as well as the unconscious, is conditioned by our particular culture. That is fairly obvious. . . . My whole being is the conscious as well as the unconscious. In the field of the unconscious are all the traditions, the residue of all the past of man, inherited as well as acquired, and in the field of the conscious I am trying to change. Such change can only be according to my conditioning, and therefore can never bring about freedom. So transformation is something which is not of the mind at all; it must be at a different level altogether, at a different depth, at a different height. . . .

So, can the mind, realizing the totality of itself, not just the superficial layers or certain depths—can the mind come to that state when transformation is not the result of a conscious or unconscious effort? If that question is clear, then the reaction to the problem arises: how is one to reach such a state? The very question *how* is another barrier. The *how* implies the search for, and practise of, a certain system, a method, the "steps" towards that fundamental, deep, inevitable transformation at a new level. . . . The *how* implies the desire to reach, the urge to achieve; and that very attempt to *be* something is the product of our society which is acquisitive, which is envious. So, we are caught again. . . .

Here is the problem: do I see that any effort I make within the field of thinking, conscious as well as unconscious, must entail a separation, a duality, and therefore conflict? If I see the truth of that, then what happens? Have I, as the conscious or unconscious mind, to do anything? Please, this is not some Oriental philosophy of doing nothing or going into some kind of mysterious trance; on the contrary, it requires a great deal of thought, penetration and inquiry. One cannot come to it unless one has gone through the whole process of understanding the conscious as well as the unconscious, not by merely saying, 'I won't think and then things will happen.' Things won't happen. That is why it is very important to have self-knowledge . . . of whatever we are—ugly, good, bad, beautiful, joyous—the whole of it; to know one's superficial conditioning as well as the deeper unconscious conditioning of centuries of tradition, of urges, compulsions, imitations; to know, to actually experience, the whole totality through self-knowledge. Then we will find that the conscious as well as the unconscious mind no longer makes any movement to achieve a change; but a change comes about, a transformation comes about at a totally different level—at a height, a depth, which the conscious and the unconscious mind can never touch. . . . And from that transformation, a different society, a different state can be brought about. But that state, that society cannot be conceived of—it must come from the depths of self-discovery. . . . Then the mind not being concerned with society, with recognition, with reformation—even with the changing of itself—finds that there *is* a change, there *is* a transformation which is not the outcome of a purposeful effort to produce a result.

London 1955: Talk #4, CW Vol. IX, pp. 55-58

Questioner: Do you work on the conscious of your listeners or on their unconscious?

Krishnamurti: What is a conscious mind and what is an unconscious mind? Please find out, do not depend upon my answer or my definition; for that you can look in a dictionary. Let us find out, let us discover the truth of the matter.

What is the conscious mind? It is the everyday mind—the everyday mind of the lawyer, the general, the policeman, the specialist; the everyday mind of acquisitive intent; the mind that is discontented and wants to find contentment; the mind that is escaping from problems; the mind that practises rituals, stupidly pursuing something rather than facing *what is*; the mind that is gregarious; the mind that is committed to a certain conclusion; the mind that is traditional, copying; the mind that is following a particular pattern of action; the conscious mind that judges, evaluates, compares, seeking its own ambitious results—that is the conscious mind of everyday activity, is it not? That mind, seeking security, may place that security on an extraordinary level; but still it is the conscious mind, whether in the bank or in *moksha* or *nirvana*. That is the conscious mind.

What is the unconscious? Do we know that there is the unconscious? . . . Are we aware that there is a whole process of the unconscious deep down, hidden, very difficult to get at? Are we aware of it? I am afraid we are not, because all our conscious effort is directed to the upper levels and there we remain—our ambitions, our social activities, our discontents, our jealousies, envies, comparing and judging—there we are. Do we know anything of the unconscious . . . except perhaps in a dream on a still night? The battles, the conflicts, are they between the unconscious and the conscious, or only between the various conscious desires? . . . Is the revolution, the total revolution, to take place at the conscious level or at a level which is not controllable by the conscious? The mind can control the conscious. If it can also control the unconscious with a view to bringing about a revolution, then it is no revolution; it is merely a conditioning of the unconscious.

We know what the conscious is; we know we live, move, function from day to day, keep going on, like a machine which is running down the hill or up the hill. When this is pointed out to you, the conscious mind then begins to watch itself. But there are hidden layers of the unconscious, which control the conscious, because the deeper layers are much more vital and much more active than the superficial mind. Is not the so-called unconscious mind the residue of all the struggles, the pursuits of all humanity, which then expresses itself outwardly, as in Hinduism with its tradition of custom and culture? . . .

Let us take, for instance, culture. Everybody is talking about it nowadays: the Eastern culture, the Indian culture, the Western culture. What does culture mean? . . . Is there such a thing as Indian culture or European culture? There may be an expression of that culture which is Indian or European. That feeling, that ecstasy, that appreciation of beauty may translate itself in a particular manner in India, in the East; the West may translate and express it in an entirely different way. But the content, the depth of feeling, is common. It is not Indian or English—which is simply stupid—though the expression may be Indian or English. So, if one wants to understand the whole process of culture, one must go into the unconscious and not into the conscious. Culture may be something not traditional at all; it must be something totally creative and not imitative. Because culture, the so-called culture, has now become traditional, we are not creative.

So, in the inquiry into what is culture, you have to go deeper and deeper. It is important to find out what the unconscious is. Do not read books. They will only *describe* what the unconscious is, and their description will prevent you from discovering it. But if you begin to inquire into it intelligently—not judging, not saying, 'This is it,' or 'That is not it,' but watching the whole process of the mind, which is meditation—then you will see that there is very little difference between the unconscious and the conscious. The conscious is merely an expression, the outward action of the unconscious. There is no gap; it is one process, the deeper process controlling the outer, shaping it, guiding it. The conflict is between the various desires in that consciousness.

The questioner wants to know if I am speaking to the conscious or the unconscious. . . . What is happening is not that I am talking to the conscious or the unconscious, but the truth is being uncovered which lies beyond the conscious and the unconscious, which means bringing about an extraordinary stillness of the mind. Do not make your minds still; do not close your eyes and become silent. Truth cannot be found by the conscious or the unconscious. Only when the mind is conscious do we know of both the conscious and the unconscious with all its workings, noises, striving. When all that comes to an end, there is stillness. This stillness is not the product of consciousness at all. It is only this stillness that is creative, that is eternal. In this stillness, that which is everlasting can be found, that comes into being. But for that silence to be, the whole process of consciousness must be understood—the workings of it, not the explanations of it. . . . That requires awareness of all things—of the trees, of the books, of people, of the smiles; of your daily mischievous actions, *pujas*, appetites, passions—of all these one must be aware. And to be aware is not to condemn, but to look at and observe them without judgement. Then only is it possible to have self-knowledge which is not taught in books, which you cannot learn by attending . . . talks. It comes into being when you watch and understand all your feelings and thoughts, from moment to moment, every day. The totality of that understanding will resolve the problems of your life.

Madras 1953: Talk #2, CW Vol. VIII, pp. 13-15

COMMON CONSCIOUSNESS

T he mind with its emotional responses, with all the things that thought has put together, is our consciousness. This consciousness with its content is the consciousness of every human being. It is modified, not entirely similar, different in its nuances and subtleties, but basically the roots of its existence are common to all of us. Gurus are playing with this consciousness for their own ends, and the scientists and psychologists are examining it. The serious ones are examining consciousness as a concept, as a laboratory process; they are examining the responses of the brain, alpha waves and so on, as something outside themselves. But we are not concerned with the theories, concepts and ideas about consciousness; we are concerned with its activity in our daily life. In understanding these activities, the daily responses, the conflicts, we will have an insight into the nature and structure of our own consciousness. As we pointed out, the basic reality of this consciousness is common to us all. It is not your particular consciousness or mine. We have inherited it, and we are modifying it, changing it here and there, but its basic movement is common to all mankind.

This consciousness is our mind with all its intricacies of thought, the emotions, the sensory responses, the accumulated knowledge, the suffering, the pain, the anxiety, the violence. All that is our consciousness. The brain is ancient and it is conditioned by centuries of evolution, by every kind of experience, increased by more recent accumulations of knowledge. All this is consciousness in action in every moment of our life. It is the relationship between humans with all the pleasures, pains, confusion of contradictory senses, and the gratification of desire with its pain. This is the movement of our life. We are asking—and this must be met as a challenge—whether this ancient movement can ever come to an end. For this has become a mechanical activity, a traditional way of life. In the ending there is a beginning, and then only is there neither ending nor beginning.

The Whole Movement of Life is Learning, pp. 85-86

THE SIGNIFICANCE OF SUBJECTS

1. History

Questioner: What is the significance of history in the education of the young?

Krishnamurti: I think if one has read history books it is fairly clear that man has struggled against nature and conquered it; now he is destroying it, polluting everything that he touches. There have been wars, killings, the Renaissance, industrialization, and man's struggle to be free. And yet he becomes a slave to institutions, organizations; he tries to break away from them but again forms another series of institutions, organizations. So, this everlasting struggle to be free—that is probably the history of mankind, according to books—and also the tribal wars, the feudal wars, the baronial wars, the wars of the kings and nations, is still going on. This tribal mind, which has become the national, sophisticated mind, is still the tribal mind.

And that, more or less, is history—perhaps we are rather simplifying it—with the culture, music, painting, the whole thing. And how is all that to be taught to the young? History is the story of mankind, the human being who has gone through all kinds of suffering, through various diseases, through wars, through religious beliefs and dogmas, persecution, the Inquisition, torture, in the name of God, in the name of peace, in the name of ideals. How is all that to be taught to the young?

If it is the story of mankind, the story of human beings, then both the educator and the young are the human beings; it is their story. It is not the story of kings and wars; it is their story, that is, the story of themselves. Now, can the educator help the student to understand the story of himself?—the story, the past, of which he is the result. Can the educator help the student to understand himself? Because he *is* the story. That is the problem.

If you are the educator and I am the student, how would you help me, as a young student, to understand the whole nature and structure of myself, myself being the whole of humanity? My brain is the result of many millions of years. How would you help me to understand myself?—my story, the past, which is all in me—the violence, the competition, the aggressiveness, the brutality, the cruelty, the fear, the pleasure, the occasional joy, and that slight perfume of love. How will you help me to understand all this? Which means the educator must also understand this. He is also understanding himself, and so helping "me", the student, to understand myself. It is a communication between the teacher and myself, and in that process of communication he is understanding himself and helping me to understand myself. . . . It is not that the teacher or the educator must first understand himself and then teach—that would take the rest of his life, perhaps—but in the relationship between the educator and the person to be educated there is a relationship of mutual investigation. Can this be done with the child, with the student? And in what manner would you set about it? That is the question.

How would you as a parent go into this? How would you help your child, your boy or girl, to understand the whole nature and structure of his mind, of his desires, of his fears, the whole momentum of life? How would you deal with it? Don't say immediately, 'We must have love,' and all that kind of stuff. It is a great problem and are we prepared as parents and teachers to bring about a new generation of people? That is what is implied: a totally different generation of people, a totally different mind and heart. Are we prepared for that? If you are a parent, would you for the sake of your daughter or son give up drink, cigarettes, pot—you know, the whole drug culture—and see that both the parent and the child are good human beings?

The word *good* means well fitted, psychologically without any friction, well fitted like a good door, like a good motor. But also *good* means whole, not broken up, not fragmented. So, are we, the elder people, prepared to bring about through education a good human being, a human being who is not afraid?—afraid of his neighbour, afraid of the future, afraid of so many things: disease, poverty, fear. Also, are we prepared in the search of the good, or in establishing the good, to help the child and ourselves to be integral? The word *integrity* means to be whole, and integrity also means to say what you mean and hold it, not say one thing and do something else. Integrity implies honesty. Are we prepared for that? Can we be honest if we have got any illusions, any romantic, speculative ideas or ideals? If we have strong beliefs, can we be honest? You may be honest to the belief, but that doesn't imply integrity. Are we prepared for all this? Or we bring children into the world, spoil them until they are 2 or 3, and then throw them to the wolves, prepare them for war. You know what is happening in the world. That's why history has not taught human beings. How many mothers must have cried, their sons being killed in wars, and yet we are incapable of stopping this monstrous movement of killing each other.

So, if you are to teach the young, one must have in oneself this sense of the demand of the good. The good is not an ideal. If we translate the good as meaning to be whole, to have integrity, to have no fear, not to be confused—these are not ideals, they are facts. So, can we be factual and so bring about a good human being through education? If we say yes, then what will the parent and you do about it? What is your responsibility? Probably you have children; if you have, then what? . . . Do we really want a different culture, a different human being with a mind that is not confused, that has no fear, that has this quality of integrity?

Ojai 1980: Q&A #1, Question 1, 6th May

2. *Mathematics*

Allan W Anderson: Might we return for a moment to education and relationship? . . . Let us say that one were fortunate enough to have a school where what you are pointing to was going on.

Krishnamurti: We are doing it, we have got seven schools.

A: It would seem that if the teacher is totally present to the child, the child will feel this; the child won't have to be instructed in what this means. Is that right?

K: Yes, but one has to find out what is the relationship of the teacher to the student. . . . Is he merely an informer, giving information to the child? Any machine can do that.

A: Oh yes, the library is filled with it.

K: Does he put himself on a pedestal, up here, and his student down there? Or is the relationship between the teacher and the student . . . a relationship in which there is learning on the part of the teacher as well as the student? Learning.

A: Yes.

K: Not, I have learned and I am going to teach you—in that, there is a division between the teacher and the student. But when there is learning on the part of the teacher as well as on the part of the student, there is no division: both are learning.

A: Yes.

K: And therefore that relationship brings about a companionship.

A: A sharing.

K: A sharing, taking a journey together, and therefore an infinite care on both sides. So, how is the teacher to teach mathematics, or whatever it is, to the student and yet teach it in such a way that you awaken the intelligence in the child, not simply about mathematics?

A: No, of course not.

K: And how do you bring this act of teaching in which there is order? Because mathematics means order: the highest form of order is mathematics. How will you convey to the student, in teaching mathematics, that there should be order in his life? Not order according to a blueprint—that's not order.

A: Yes, yes.

K: It is a creative teaching. . . . It's an act of learning all the time—it's a living thing—not something I have learnt and I am going to impart to you.

A: This reminds me of a little essay I read many years ago by Simone Weil which she called *On Academic Studies,* or some title like that, and she said that everyone who teaches a subject is responsible for teaching the student the relation between what they are studying and the student's making a pure act of attention.

K: I know, of course.

A: And that if this doesn't take place, the whole thing doesn't mean a thing. When one stops to think what a teacher would say if a student walked up and looked at them and said, 'Fine, we're studying calculus right now. Now, you tell me how I am to see this that I am pursuing, in relation to my making a pure act of attention'—it would be likely a little embarrassing, except for the most unusual person who has a grasp of the present.

K: So, sir, that's just it. What is the relationship of the teacher to the student in education? Is he training him merely to conform, is he training him to cultivate mere memory like a machine? Is he training, or is he helping him to learn about life . . . about the whole immensity of living, the complexity of it?

A Wholly Different Way of Living, pp. 62-63

RIGHT ACTION

We are asking what place has knowledge when there is an inquiry into right action. Right action means correct action, accurate action, precise action—not right action according to you or me, or action based on some pattern, some conclusion, some ideal. Those are not actually correct action. So we are trying to find out, if you are interested in it—and you must be, as a human being, when there is so much confusion, both outwardly and inwardly—what place has knowledge with regard to right action? We have got tremendous knowledge, and knowledge implies, by the very word, that which has been known, which has been acquired, which has been accumulated through experience, through education and so on. There are scientists saying man can ascend only through knowledge: the ascent of man through acquiring more and more knowledge.

Knowledge is always in the past. There is no knowledge of tomorrow. The "tomorrow" is dictated by the knowledge of yesterday, passing through the present. So we live in the past, if you observe yourself. You might have had a marvellous experience a couple of years ago, or yesterday, and that experience, the residue of that beauty or that love—whatever it is you think that experience was—is gone and you are searching for it, longing for it; longing which again is in the field of knowledge, always functioning within the field of the known.

So, what is right action? What is right action which will be true, precise, accurate, correct under all circumstances?—whether you are at home, in the office, whatever you are doing. It is very important to find out. Does knowledge bring order? Action, correct action, is based on order not of choice, not on accumulated information called knowledge. . . . Knowledge implies the storing up of experience, gathering all the known facts, storing them up in the brain and acting according to memory. That is simple: acting according to memory. Does acting according to that bring order? Please be clear on this point. We are investigating; I am not telling you it does or it does not. But through exploring, investigating, we'll find out whether knowledge, which is always the past, can bring about order.

Madras 1977: Talk #3, 31st December

I wonder if you ever ask yourself a fundamental question, a question that in the very asking indicates a depth of seriousness, a question the answering of which does not necessarily depend on another, or on any philosophy, teacher and so on. I would like to ask one of those serious and fundamental questions.

Is there an action which is right under all circumstances? Or is there only action, neither right nor wrong? Does right action vary according to the individual and the different circumstances in which he is placed? The individual, as opposed to the community. The individual as a soldier might ask, 'What is right action?' To him, as he is at the front, the "right action" obviously would be to kill. And the individual with his family, enclosed within the four walls of the idea of "mine"—*my* family, *my* possessions—to him there is also right action. And the businessman in the office, to him also there is right action. And so, right action breeds opposition, individual action opposed to collective action. Each maintains that his action is right. The religious man with his exclusive beliefs and dogmas pursues what he considers right action, and this separates him from the non-believer, from those who think or feel the opposite of what he believes. There is the action of the specialist who is working according to certain specialized knowledge; he says, 'This is the right action.' There are politicians with their right and wrong action: the communists, the socialists, the capitalists and so on. There is this whole stream of life which includes the business life, the political life, the religious life, the life of the family, and also the life in which there is beauty, love, kindliness, generosity and so on. One asks, in looking at all these fragmentary actions which breed their own opposites: what is right action in all circumstances? Or there is only action, which is neither right nor wrong?—a very difficult statement to make or to believe, because obviously it is wrong action to kill; obviously it is wrong action when one is held by a particular dogma and acts according to that.

There are those who, seeing all this, say, 'We are activists; we are not concerned with philosophies, with theories, with various forms of speculative ideology; we are concerned with action, doing.' And there are those who withdraw from doing into monasteries; they retire into themselves and go to some paradise of their own, or they spend years in meditation, thinking to find the truth, and from there act.

So, observing these phenomena, the opposing and fragmentary actions of those who say, 'We are right; this is right action; this will solve the problems of the world,' yet creating, consciously or unconsciously, activities opposed to that, and thus everlasting divisions and aggressive attitudes, one asks, what is one to do? What is one to do in a world that is really appalling, brutal, a world where there is such violence, such corruption?—where money, money, money matters enormously and where one is willing to sacrifice another in seeking power, position, prestige, fame; where each man is struggling to assert, to fulfil, to *be* somebody. What is one to do? What are *you* to do?

I do not know if you have asked this question. What am I, living in this world, seeing all this before me—the misery, the enormous suffering man is inflicting upon man, the deep suffering that one goes through, the anxiety, the fear, the sense of guilt, the hope and the despair—seeing all this, one must, if one is at all aware, ask: what am I, living in this world, to do? How would you answer that question? If you put that question to yourself in all seriousness, if you put that question very, very seriously, it has an extraordinary intensity and immediacy. What is your answer to this challenge? One sees that the fragmentary action, the action that is "right", does lead to contradiction, to opposition, to separateness. Man has pursued this "right action", calling it morality, pursuing a behaviour pattern, a system in which he is caught and by which he is conditioned; to him there is right action and wrong action, which in their turn produce other contradictions and oppositions. So one asks oneself: is there an action which is neither right nor wrong—only action?

Saanen 1968: Talk #5, 16th July
1968 Talks and Dialogues

EXCELLENCE

I t is necessary to go into the question of what order is, and why the mind, the brain, has not been able to function in an orderly way. Our education, whether in the West or in the East, North or South, is making human beings mediocre. I mean by that word, following a routine, fitting into a slot, whether it is an administrative slot, a surgical slot, or the slot of a lawyer or an engineer. We are all being educated to conform to a pattern, whether that pattern be highly paid, highly respected, or a pattern that may be socially convenient, profitable, and perhaps worthwhile. I do not know if you have examined your own minds, your own activities, and discovered for yourself, if one may be so presumptuous, whether your brains—and therefore your whole series of chain reactions— have not conformed, have not followed a pattern, have not become a machine of identification, conformity, imitation, whether it be religious, political, economic, social and so on.

It is very important to find out why we have not become excellent—I am going to use that word *excellent* very carefully—excellent not in profession, not in a career—there are thousands of people, perhaps millions, throughout the world who are very, very efficient, who are earning a great deal of money—but we are talking about the mediocrity of a brain that refuses to alter the pattern in which it is caught. The brain becomes dull, it hasn't got the rapidity or freedom in which it can see its own movement. Most of us are frightened of freedom—not the rebellion that takes place against the establishment; that's only a reaction which pushes you in the opposite direction: permissiveness, drugs and all that business—we are afraid to be radically, deeply, free of mediocrity. We want to be very safe both outwardly and inwardly. This search for certainty is a form of mediocrity, wanting to be successful as an artist, as a lawyer, as an engineer and so on.

Excellence is not achieved through competition: excellence in aesthetics, in the appreciation and the perception of that which is beautiful, excellence in morality—morality in the sense of conduct, behaviour, a sense of dignity—which freedom brings. When one looks at the world, as you must— not the little world around oneself, of the office, of the factory, the family, the happenings of the politicians and so on, but the world in which human beings are suffering, the world in which almost everyone has a great sense of anxiety, sorrow, pain—nothing to do with any kind of career or religious belief, it is actually going on in the world—when one regards all that, why has the brain—which has been capable of such extraordinary activity in the technological world—why has it become sluggish; why, though it is capable of action in a certain direction, is it incapable of perceiving the whole structure and the nature of man and acting from that? One would call a mediocre person one who is incapable of such perception. . . .

The computer is going to take over our brains. I do not know if you are aware of this. The robot and the computer are going to manage factories, the manual labour and so on.

And so, if one is not aware of all this, our brains are going to become more and more sluggish because there will be no physical problems, technological problems, but there will be psychological problems. Even that, perhaps, the computer will take over because we will be just human beings without any occupation, empty, sluggish. This is coming, perhaps within the next fifteen or twenty years. So, what does education mean?

Madras 1980-81: Talk #4, 4th January

Most people are "diligent" in their own self-interest, whether that self-interest is identified with the family, with a particular group, sect, or nation. In this self-interest there is the seed of negligence, although there is constant preoccupation with oneself. This preoccupation is limited and so it is negligence. This preoccupation is energy held within a narrow boundary. Diligence is freedom from self-occupation and brings an abundance of energy. When one understands the nature of negligence, the other comes into being without any struggle. When this is fully understood—not just the verbal definitions of negligence and diligence—then the highest excellence in our thought, action, behaviour will manifest itself.

But unfortunately we never demand of ourselves the highest quality of thought, action and behaviour. We hardly ever challenge ourselves, and if we ever do, we have various excuses for not responding fully. Doesn't this indicate an indolence of mind, the feeble activity of thought? The body can be lazy, but never the mind with its quickness of thought and subtlety. Laziness of the body can easily be understood. This laziness may be because one is overworked or has overindulged, or has played sport too hard. So the body requires rest—which may be considered laziness, though it is not. The watchful mind, being alert, sensitive, knows when the organism needs rest and care.

The Whole Movement of Life is Learning, pp. 32-33

We are dealing with the facts of daily life, our way of living. Most of us abstract from those facts ideas and conclusions which become our prisons. We may ventilate those prisons, but still we live there and go on making further abstractions of facts there. We are not dealing with ideas, exotic philosophies, or with abstract conclusions. We are going into problems that require a great deal of care and about which we must be very serious—because the house is burning. . . . If you are aware of the world situation, of what is happening in the world economically, socially, politically, of the preparation for wars, you become extremely serious; it is not a thing to play around with, you have to act.

Most of us are mediocre. The word *mediocre* means to go halfway up the hill. We all do that—we just go halfway up the hill. Excellence means going to the very top of it, and we are asking for excellence; otherwise we shall be smothered, destroyed as human beings, by the politicians, by the ideologists, whether they are communists, socialists, and so on. We are demanding of ourselves the highest form of excellence. That excellence can only come into being when there is clarity and compassion, without which the human mind will destroy human beings, destroy the world.

We are exercising reason, clear objective thinking, and logic, but they themselves do not bring about compassion. We must exercise the qualities that we have, which are reason, careful observation, and from those the excellency of clear sight to examine the various contents of consciousness, in which compassion does not exist. There may be pity in them, sympathy and tolerance, there may be the desire to help, there may be a form of love; but all these are not compassion.

The Wholeness of Life, p. 167

EDUCATION AND REVOLUTION

I s it not important for each one of us to find out what education implies, the total education of man? If we can find out not as a group of people but as individuals what this education implies, what the principles of this total education of man are, we can create a different world. We see that so far no form of revolution has produced peace in the world—even the communist revolution has not brought about great benefit to man—nor has any organized religion brought peace to man. Organized religions may give an illusory peace to the mind, but real peace between man and man has not been produced. So, is it not very important for each one of us to find out how to improve this state of affairs?

We may pass examinations, we may have various kinds of jobs, but in an overpopulated world where there are so many linguistic and religious divisions, there is always a threatening of wars, there is no security, everything about us is disintegrating. In order to solve this problem, is it not important to inquire—not superficially, not argumentatively, not by putting one nation against another or one idea against another—and to find out, each one of us, the truth of the matter? Truth is entirely different from information, from knowledge. Neither battles nor the latest atomic weapons nor the totalitarian systems of thought, either political or religious, have solved anything. So we, you and I, cannot rely on any system or any opinion, but must really try to find out for ourselves what the whole purpose of being educated is. After all, that is what we are concerned with.

Does education cease when you pass an examination and have a job? Is it not a continual process at all the different levels and processes of our consciousness, of our being, throughout life? That requires not mere assertion of information, but real understanding. Every religion, every schoolteacher, every political system tells us what to do, what to think, what to hope for. But is it not now very important that each one of us should think out these problems for ourselves and be a light to ourselves? That is the real need of the present time—how to be a light to ourselves, how to be free from all the authoritative, hierarchical attitude to life, so that each one of us is a light to oneself. To be that, it is very important to find out how to *be*, how to let that light come into being.

So, is it not the function of education to help man to bring about a total revolution? Most of us are concerned with partial revolution, economic or social. But the revolution of which I am talking is a total revolution of man at all the levels of his consciousness, of his life, of his being. But that requires a great deal of understanding. It is not the result of any theory or any system of thought; on the contrary, no system of thought can produce a revolution: it can only produce a particular effect, which is not a revolution. The revolution which is essential at the present time can only come into being when there is a total apprehension of the process in which man's mind works—not according to any particular religion or any particular philosophy, like Marxism, or any system, like the capitalist system—the understanding of ourselves as a total process. That is the only revolution that can bring about lasting peace.

Varanasi 1954: Talk #1, CW, Vol. VIII, pp. 141-42

LOVE AND COMPASSION

Thought is memory, experience and knowledge, and this memory with its images and its shadows is the self, the "me" and the "not me", "we" and "they". The essence of division is the self with all its attributes and qualities. Materialism only gives strength and growth to the self. The self may and does identify itself with the State, with an ideology, with activities of the "non-me", religious or secular, but it is still the self. Its beliefs are self-created, as are its pleasures and fears. Thought by its very nature and structure is fragmentary, and conflict and war are between the various fragments: the nationalities, the races, the ideologies. A materialistic humanity will destroy itself unless the self is wholly abandoned. The abandonment of the self is always of primary importance. And only from this revolution can a new society be put together.

The abandonment of the self is love, compassion, passion for all things: the starving, the suffering, the homeless, and for the materialist and the believer. Love is not sentimentality, romanticism; it is as strong and final as death.

Krishnamurti's Journal, p. 78

It is a great thing to understand suffering, because where there is freedom from sorrow there is compassion. One is not compassionate as long as one is anchored to any belief, to any particular form of religious symbol. Compassion is freedom from sorrow. Where there is compassion there is love. With that compassion goes intelligence—not the intelligence of thought with its cunning, with its adjustments, with its capacity to put up with anything. Compassion means the ending of sorrow, and only then is there intelligence.

The Network of Thought, pp. 97- 98

LOVE, COMPASSION AND WISDOM

I s love pleasure? . . . Pleasure always invites fear; and is pleasure love, is pleasure desire, is desire love? The remembrance of something pleasurable that happened yesterday, is that love? We are caught in that circle. Don't agree or disagree but watch yourself and you will see that we are caught in that area. Every human being is caught in that. The ambitious man driven by his desire to become something in the political field or in the business field—whatever field he wants to succeed in—can such a man love? He may talk about it endlessly but he does not know love. You are also in that field; you may nod your head and agree, but you haven't left that field though you verbally agree. You are living on words, and therefore degeneracy is settling in your heart and mind.

Knowledge is words. Knowledge is not wisdom. You can't buy wisdom. You can attend any school where they teach you knowledge, but there is no book, there is no school where wisdom can be taught. If there is such a school, scrap it, don't go near it. Wisdom comes when you understand what love is, the enormous compassion, and that compassion can come only when you understand the depth of suffering and when you understand the content of your consciousness, which is yourself. The content of that consciousness *is* yourself, and in the understanding of yourself flowers wisdom.

Madras 1974: Talk #2
Talks in India 1974-75, pp. 19-20

SILENCE AND MEDITATION

Having laid the foundation, not as an idea, not as a concept, not as an abstraction, but in actual daily life, we can then begin to inquire if there is something more which is not of time, which cannot be destroyed. To find out, or rather to come upon it, we must understand meditation. I am sorry to introduce that word because it has been spoilt by those people who have recently come from the East talking about meditation. Unless the mind is very still, you cannot see anything—that is a simple psychological fact. If I want to see you or you want to see me actually, physically, your mind must be very quiet; it cannot be chattering or indulging in images, opinions, judgements: it must be absolutely quiet. Most of our minds do not even know what that word means, or what lies behind it. We have a feeling that there must be a certain stillness of the mind; after all, if you are listening to the speaker—and I hope you are—you must give attention, that is, your mind must not be out playing golf, your mind must be wondering what he means, and your mind must not only be quiet but attentive. When it is attentive it is intense; then there is a communion between the speaker and yourself, a communion that is intense, a meeting of his mind and yours, at the same time, with the same intensity and at the same level. Then there is real communion. And for that your mind must be extraordinarily sensitive, alert, quiet.

The word *meditation* is very common throughout the whole of Asia. They practise what they call meditation—one sees poor men, ill-clad and ill-fed, sitting under a tree meditating, the body motionless—that has been going on for thousands of years. In that so-called meditation there is no order in the sense we mean, the order which comes with freedom from tradition, from imitation, from fear: there is only conformity to a pattern. Those who meditate want wider, deeper experiences which can very easily be gained through the psychedelic drugs that give you an expansion of consciousness, but that expansion of consciousness is still conditioned. So, meditation is something entirely different, and unless there is a foundation of order, freedom and love which has never touched brutality, it is not possible. Then the mind becomes the meditative mind and therefore completely quiet, not wanting any pleasure, experiences or visions. Visions, as the Christian seeing Christ or the Hindu with his Krishna, are very simple to explain: they are projections arising out of the conditioning of the mind. In the same way, the communist has his vision of what the State should be or what the citizen should be, according to his conditioning. It is fairly easy to have visions, but whether you see Christ, the Buddha or Krishna, they have really no meaning whatsoever; they are the result of your own psychological state. When you have these visions, the more you are caught, the more you are conditioned. So all that is not meditation.

Meditation is the silence of the mind; but in that silence, in that intensity, in that total alertness, the mind is no longer the seat of thought, because thought is time, thought is memory, thought is knowledge. When it is completely quiet and highly sensitive, the mind can take a voyage which is timeless, limitless. That is meditation, not all this stupid nonsense of repeating words, which is what they are doing. In India it is a well-known trick, repeating a word and thereby getting oneself into a peculiar state and thinking that is meditation. You can repeat the words *Coca Cola* ten thousand times and you will have the most marvellous experience because you have hypnotized yourself, but that is not reality. Hypnosis, whether it is done by yourself or by another, can only project your own conditioning, your own anxieties and fears. It has no value whatsoever.

So, is it possible for a mind that has penetrated deeply into this problem of order to live in the world with that and act from that? To live with order and the beauty of order—order which is not habit but which dies every day and therefore each day it is new—to live with a quality of love that has no fear, that is never touched by thought as pleasure. This is really the main issue, not what you believe or do not believe, whether you are a communist, a socialist or a nationalist—we have finished and done with all that. It has never produced order in the world; on the contrary, it has divided man more and more.

Talks in Europe 1968, pp. 41-43

Meditation is unpremeditated art. . . . You can't prepare for meditation. There is no system, no method. . . . We can banish all the systems, all the methods, the postures, the breathing, forcing the mind and thought to be controlled and so on. The controller *is* the controlled. Thought creates the controller and then the controller says it must control thought in order to meditate, which is obviously silly. . . .

So, we are going to find out what meditation is. Not *how* to meditate but the depth and the beauty and the reality and immense possibility of meditation. The word means to ponder, think over, be concerned—the dictionary meaning of that word—but the word is not the thing. The word *meditation* is not meditation. And why should one meditate at all? Is meditation separate from life? Our daily living—the office, the family, sex, the pursuit of ambition—is that separate from meditation? Or is meditation part of life? If it is separate and you meditate in order to live a better life, in order to be better, then you are imposing certain concepts on actuality, certain experiences, essentially of others, on what you think should happen. To deny all that . . . is to deny everything that man has thought—about meditation, about silence, about truth, about eternity, whether there is a timeless state and so on—to be free of other people's knowledge completely. And that goes very, very far. . . . To deny your gods, your sacred books, your tradition, your beliefs—everything wiped away—because you understand they are the result of thought. Which means you are totally, psychologically, not dependent on anything. . . . You are free of fear, no longer touched by sorrow; which does not mean that you become hard, bitter, cruel.

Without love and compassion there is no meditation. So, living every day in this world which is corrupt beyond words . . . living in this world, surrounded by all this, to have that sense of total, absolute freedom because you have denied everything that man has thought out, except the technological world. . . . Then you enter into quite a different dimension—not *you* enter—there *is* the mind. The mind is entirely different from the brain. And that mind cannot be understood, known or perceived unless the brain with all its sensory responses is understood. Which means to see something—the sea, a sheet of water, or anything of nature—with all your senses, not merely with your eyes; to hear one thing with all your senses. When you perceive with all your senses there is no recording, there is no "I"; it is only when we perceive something partially that the partial perceiving creates the "me" which is partial.

So, when the brain is totally free from all accumulated psychological knowledge, then there is the mind. I won't go into that, then it becomes a theory. . . . Unless one has done all this actually—you can test it, you can see it in your daily life—it isn't worth it. So, when there is this absolute denial of all the psychological accumulation, then the brain becomes quiet, it hasn't to be induced to be quiet. Then illumination is not an experience. Illumination means to see things clearly, as they are, and to go beyond them.

Madras 1981: Talk #6, 11ᵗʰ January

MEDITATION WITH SCHOOL STUDENTS

D o you know anything about meditation? You are interested in sex, you are interested in being entertained; you are interested in learning geography, history; interested casually in many things. Meditation is part of life—don't say it is something outside of life for some silly people—it is part of existence. So you must know about it as you must know about mathematics, electronics or whatever it is. Do you know what it means to meditate? The dictionary meaning of the word is to ponder, to think over, to ruminate, to inquire into.

When you sit very quietly, or lie down very quietly, the body is completely relaxed, isn't it? Have you ever tried to sit very, very quietly—not to force it because the moment you force it, it is finished—to sit very quietly, either with your eyes closed or open? If you have your eyes open there is a little more distraction, you begin to see things. After looking at things—the curve of the tree, the leaves, the bushes—after looking at it all with care, then close your eyes; then you will not say to yourself, 'What is happening, let me look.' First look at everything—the furniture, the colour of the chair, the colour of the sweater—look at the shape of the tree. After having looked, the desire to look out is less: I have seen that blue sky and I have finished with it and I will not look again. But first you must look, then you can sit quietly. When you sit quietly or lie down very quietly, the blood flows easily into your head. There is no strain. That is why they say you must sit cross-legged, with head very straight, because the blood flows easier that way. If you sit crouched, it is more difficult for the blood to go into the head. So, you sit or lie down very, very quietly. Don't force it, don't fidget. If you fidget then watch it; don't say, 'I must not.' Then, when you sit very quietly, you watch your mind. First you watch the mind. Don't correct it, don't say, 'This thought is good, that thought is not good'— just watch it. Then you will see that there is a watcher and the watched; there is a division. The moment there is a division there is conflict.

Now, can you watch without the watcher? Is there a watching without the watcher? It is the watcher that says, 'This is good and that is bad,' 'This I like and that I don't like,' or, 'I wish she hadn't said this or that,' 'I wish I had more food.' Watch without the watcher. Try it some time. That is part of meditation—just begin with that—that's good enough. You will see, if you have done it, what an extraordinary thing takes place. . . . Your body becomes very, very intelligent. Now the body is not intelligent because we have spoiled it. We have destroyed the natural intelligence of the body itself. Then you will find that the body says, 'Go to bed at the right time'—it wants it. It has its own intelligence and activity. And also if it wants to be lazy, let it be lazy.

You try it. When I come back here, we'll sit down together twice a week and go into all this, shall we? Good! I feel you ought to leave this place highly intelligent—not just pass some exams, but be tremendously intelligent, aware, beautiful persons. At least, that is how I feel for you.

Beginnings of Learning, pp. 79-80

MEDITATION AND EDUCATION

C an we go into the question of meditation as a comprehensive, total approach to life?—which implies the understanding of what meditation is. I do not know if any of you meditate, and I do not know what meditation means to you. What part has meditation in education, and what do we mean by meditation? We give so much importance to the getting of a degree, the getting of a job, to financial security: that is the entire design of our thinking. And meditation, the real inquiry into whether there is God—the observing, experiencing, of that immeasurable state—is not part of our education at all. We will have to find out what we mean by meditation. Not how to meditate—that is an immature way of looking at meditation. If one can unravel what is meditation, then the very process of unravelling is meditation.

What is meditation, and what is thinking? If we inquire into what meditation is, we have to inquire into what thinking is; otherwise merely to meditate when I do not know the process of thinking is to create a fancy, a delusion, which has no reality whatsoever. So, to really understand or to discover what meditation is, it is not enough to have mere explanations, which are only verbal and therefore have little significance: one has to go into the whole process of thinking.

Thinking is a response of memory. Thoughts become the slave of words, the slave of symbols, of ideas; and the mind is the word, and the mind becomes slave to words like *God, communist, the principal, the vice-principal, the prime minister, the police inspector, the villager, the cook.* See the nuances of these words and the feelings that accompany these words. You say *sannyasi* and immediately there is a certain quality of respect. So the word, for most of us, has immense significance. For most of us, the mind *is* the word. Within the conditioned, verbal, technical, symbolic framework we live and think. That framework is the past, which is time. If you observe this process taking place in yourself, then it has significance.

Now, is there thought without word? Is there thinking without word and therefore out of time? The word is time. If the mind can separate the word, the symbol, from itself, then is there an inquiry which does not seek an end and is therefore timeless? First let us look at the whole picture. A mind that has no space in which to observe has no quality of perception. From thinking, there is no observation. Most of us see through words, and is that seeing? When I see a flower and say it is a rose, do I see the rose or do I see the feeling, the idea that the word invokes? So can the mind, which is of time and space, explore into a non-spatial, timeless state? It is only in that state that there is creation. A technical mind which has acquired specialized knowledge can invent, add to, but it can never create. A mind that has no space, no emptiness from which to see, is obviously a mind that is incapable of living in a spaceless, timeless state. That is what is demanded. So, a mind that is merely caught in time and space, in words, in itself, in conclusions, in techniques, in specialization, such a mind is a very distressed mind. When the world is confronted with something totally new, all our old answers, codes and traditions are inadequate.

What is thinking? Most of our lives are spent in the effort to *be* something, to become something, to achieve something. Most of our lives are a series of connected and disconnected efforts, and in these efforts the whole problem of ambition and contradiction brings about a certain exclusive process which we call concentration. Why should we make an effort? What is the point of effort? Would we stagnate if we failed to make an effort? What does it matter if we stagnate? Are we not stagnating with our immense efforts now? What significance has effort anymore? If the mind understands effort, will it not release a different kind of energy which does not think in terms of achievement, ambition and so contradiction? Is not that very energy action itself?

In effort there is involved idea and action, and the problem of how to bridge idea and action. All effort implies idea and action, and the coming together of these two. Why should there be such division? Is not such a division destructive? All divisions are contradictory, and in the self-contradictory state there is inattention. The greater the contradiction, the greater the inattention, and the greater the resultant action. So, life is an endless battle from the moment we are born to the moment we die.

Is it possible to educate both ourselves and the students to live? I do not mean to live merely as an intellectual being, but as a complete human being, having a good body and a good mind, enjoying nature, seeing the totality: the misery, the love, the sorrow, the beauty of the world.

When we consider what meditation is, I think one of the first things is the quietness of the body, a quietness that is not enforced, sought after. I do not know if you have noticed a tree blowing in the wind, and the same tree in the evening when the sun has set? It is quiet. In the same way, can the body be quiet, naturally, normally, healthily? All this implies an inquiring mind which is not seeking a conclusion or starting from a motive. How is a mind to inquire into the unknown, the immeasurable? How is one to inquire into God? That is also part of meditation. How do we help the student to probe into all this? Machines and electronic brains are taking over; automation is going to come in about fifty years and you will have leisure and you can turn to books for knowledge. Our intelligence—not merely the capacity to reason, but rather the capacity to perceive, understand what is true and what is false—is being destroyed by the emphasis on authority, acceptance, imitation, in which is security. All this is going on, but in all this what part has meditation? I feel the quality of meditation as I am talking to you. It *is* meditation. I am talking but the mind that is communing is in a state of meditation.

All this implies an extraordinarily pliable mind, not a mind that accepts, rejects, acquiesces or conforms. So, meditation is the unfolding of the mind and through it perception, the seeing without restraint, without a background, and so an endless emptiness in which to see. The seeing without the limitation of thought, which is time, requires a mind that is astonishingly quiet, still.

All this implies an intelligence which is not the result of education, book learning, acquisition of techniques. To observe a bird you must be very quiet; otherwise at the least movement on your part the bird flies away. The whole of your body must be quiet, relaxed, sensitive to see. How do you create that feeling? Take that one thing, which is part of meditation. How will you bring this about in a school like this? First of all, is it necessary at all to observe, to think, to have a mind that is subtle, a mind that is still, a body that is responsive, sensitive, eager?

We are only concerned with helping the student to get a degree and to get a job, and then we allow him to sink into this monstrous society. To help him to be alive, it is imperative for a student to have this extraordinary feeling for life—not his life or somebody else's life, but for life—for the villager, for the tree. That is part of meditation: to be passionate about it, to love, which demands a great sense of humility. This humility is not to be cultivated. Now, how will you create the climate for this? Because children are not born perfect. You may say that all we have to do is to create the environment and they will grow into marvellous beings. They will not. They are what they are, the result of our past with all our anxieties and fears; and we have created the society in which they live, and children have to adjust themselves and are conditioned by us. How will you create the climate in which they see all these influences, in which they look at the beauty of this earth, look at the beauty of this valley? Just as you devote time to mathematics, science, music, dance, why do you not give some time to all this?

Teacher: I was thinking about practical difficulties, and how it is not always possible.

Krishnamurti: Why do you give time to dance, to music? Why not give time to this, as you give to mathematics? You are not interested in it. If you saw that it was also necessary, you would devote time to it. If you saw that it was as essential as mathematics, you would do something.

Meditation implies the whole of life, not just the technical, monastic or scholastic life but total life; and to apprehend and communicate this totality there must be a certain seeing of it without space and time. A mind must have, in itself, a sense of the spaceless and the timeless state. It must see the whole of the picture. How will you approach it and help the student to see the whole of life—not in little segments but life in its totality? I want him to comprehend the enormity of this.

Krishnamurti on Education, pp. 171-77

SOURCE NOTES

The Purpose of Life
- 'Does life have a meaning...because love *is* God.'
  From *The First and Last Freedom*, pp. 280-81.
- 'The Questioner...when his desire is still.'
  From *Collected Works Vol. IV* pp. 129-30.

Education and the Purpose of Life
- 'What is right...there be right education?'
  From *Collected Works Vol. VI* pp. 20-22.

The Aims of Education
- 'The ignorant man...systems and beliefs.'
  From *Education and the Significance of Life* pp. 17-25.
- 'To really tackle...penetration, meditation.'
  From *Collected Works Vol. VIII* p. 227.

Educating the Educator
- 'May we know...efficiency of machinery.'
  From *Collected Works Vol. IV* pp.106-08.

The Individual and Society

- 'The modern educational...integrated human being.'
  From *Commentaries on Living Series II* pp. 46-47.
- 'It not important...creative human beings.'
  From *Collected Works Vol. IX* p. 9.

Fear, Anxiety, Emptiness

- 'We are asking...move away from it.'
  From *Truth and Actuality* pp.75-76.

Emptiness, Loneliness, Sorrow, Death

- 'This is not...This is a fact.'
  From *Collected Works Vol. XI* p. 286.

Being Alone With Death

- 'To come upon...outside of all that?'
  From *The Wholeness of Life* pp. 210-11.

The Conditioning Process

- 'If the totality...the immeasurable.'
  From *Collected Works Vol. X* pp.50-51.
- 'The problem is...liberation from conditioning.'
  From *Collected Works Vol. VI* pp.109-10.

Education and the Conditioning Process

- 'The child is...without conditioning.'
  From *Education and the Significance of Life* pp. 27-29.

Relationship of the Teacher with the Student

- 'One has to...both are learning.'
  From *A Wholly Different Way of Living* pp. 62-63.

- 'I would like...to work together.'
  From Brockwood 1979: Conversation with Teachers #3, 23rd June. (*KFT Bulletin #73*)

The Child and the Adult
- 'Most children are...to discover the real.'
  From *Education and the Significance of Life*, pp. 41-46.

The Observation of Relationship
- 'The next question...what happens?'
  From *On Learning and Knowledge*, pp. 69-70.

Relationship with the World and People
- 'All your religions...what we are doing.'
  From Rajghat 1981: Talk 1, 25th November.
- 'There must be order...which is it?'
  From *The Awakening of Intelligence*, pp. 311-12.

Relationship to Nature (Working with One's Hands)
- 'What is the meaning...challenges of life.'
  From *Collected Works Vol. V*, pp. 142-43.

The Integrated Human Being
- 'The Professor had...integration comes into being.'
  From *Commentaries on Living: Series II*, pp. 46-47, 51.
- 'I love my son...property and with ideas.'
  From *Collected Works Vol. VI* p. 236-37.

The Integrated Human Being (The Role of the Educator)
- 'What do we mean...would be right education.'
  From *Collected Works Vol. VII*, pp. 157-60.

Brain and Mind

- 'For most of us…from the brain.'
  From Ojai 1981: Talk 1, 2nd May.
- 'How do you explain…observe the unconscious?'
  From *The Flight of the Eagle, pp. 21-22.*
- 'I think the mind…body or the brain.'
  From *The Future of Humanity*, pp. 57-58.

Knowledge, Memory, Experience, Thinking

- 'Wh*at is though…its own* division.'
  From Saanen 1982: Talk 2, 13th July.
- 'The central problem…war with each other.'
  From Saanen 1972: Talk 3, 20th July.
- 'Our consciousness is…the other direction?'
  From Brockwood 1981: Talk 1, 29th August.

Thought process, Ego process

- 'To understand relationship…understanding of relationship.'
  From *Collected Works Vol. VI*, p. 91.
- 'Relationship can only…in all relationship.'
  From *Talks in Europe 1968.*

Identity and Identification

- 'Why do you identify…comes into being.'
  From *Commentaries on Living Series I*, pp. 11-13.
- 'How can individual…complex and vast problem.'
  From *Collected Works Vol. VI*, pp. 296-97.
- 'We must re-educate ourselves…goodwill and peace.'
  From *Collected Works Vol. III*, pp. 242-43.

Concentration, Awareness and Attention
- 'For the most of…it is limited.'
  From Ojai 1982: Q&A 2, 6th May.
- 'To be choicelessly…no seeing at all.'
  From *Collected Works Vol. XIII*, pp. 201-02.

Listening, Looking, Learning
- 'If one listens…looking at the fact.'
  From *Collected Works Vol. XV*, p. 135.
- 'A boy in a class…which is not conformity.'
  From *Collected Works Vol. XIV*, p. 240.

Freedom
- 'Revolt is not freedom…comes freedom and order.'
  From *Collected Works Vol. XVI*.
- 'Learning about oneself…there is freedom.'
  From *Talks in Europe 1967*.
- 'Life is a thing…true religious revolution.'
  From *Collected Works Vol. VIII*, p. 183.

Freedom and Order in School
- 'You cannot have…going to class.'
  From *Krishnamurti on Education*, pp. 30-33.

Fear and Authority in School
- 'What place has…wherever you are.'
  From *The Whole Movement of Life is Learning, p. 173*.
- 'Should you not…any scholastic degree.'
  From *Life Ahead*, pp. 95-97.

Insight
- 'What is the nature...beginning another day.'
  From *Fire in the Mind*, pp. 260-63.
- 'Are we saying that...from our childhood?'
  From *The Ending of Time*, pp. 161-65.

Inquiry and Investigation
- 'To explore there...ways of your thought.'
  From *Collected Works Vol. XIII*, pp. 113, 115, 117, 118.
- 'What is that thing...investigate, be innocent.'
  From *Collected Works Vol. XI*, pp. 63-64, 65 & 66.

Investigation with School Students
- 'It is very important...its own superficial activities.'
  From *Collected Works Vol. VIII*, pp.119-20 & 122.

Comparison and Competition
- 'Most people think...the work of the educator.'
  From *Life Ahead* (Introduction).
- 'Almost all human beings...a quality as dullness.'
  From *The Whole Movement Of Life is Learning*, pp. 101-02.
- 'We are always...to any party.'
  From *Talks and Dialogues Saanen 1967*, p. 23.
- 'How can one be...its own heights.'
  From *Collected Works Vol. VIII*, p. 134.

Harmony of Body, Mind and Heart
- 'I want to find out...Is this possible?'
  From *Exploration into Insight*, p. 52.
- 'We live by our...be awakened?'
  From *The Whole Movement Of Life is Learning*, pp. 80-82.

Thinking Together
- 'It is important...of all humanity.'
  From *The Network of Thought pp. 84-85.*
- 'I hope we can...as two friends.'
  From Ojai 1980: Talk 3, 10th May.

Thinking Together about Education
- 'What are your...right kind of education.'
  From *Collected Works Vol. X*, pp. 64-65.

Negative Thinking
- 'Negative thinking...any prejudice or conclusion.'
  From *Collected Works Vol. XI*, p. 329.
- 'One begins...the religious spirit.'
  From *Collected Works Vol. XII*, pp. 170-71.

Intelligence
- 'About intelligence, I always...I know.'
  From *The Awakening of Intelligence*, pp. 509-11.
- 'Our minds are the...we are acting.'
  From Madras 1979: Talk 2, 23rd December.
- 'We have seen that...insight brings order.'
  From Ojai 1978: Talk 2, 2nd April.

Intelligence, Global Thinking and Education
- 'It is important...conditioned it is.'
  From *Collected Works Vol. VIII*, pp. 226-27.

Intelligence and Cleverness
- 'Is there any difference...not a clever person.'
  From *Collected Works Vol. VIII*, p. 75

The Scientific Mind and the Religious Mind
- 'A religious mind…at all times.'
  From *Collected Works Vol. XII*, p. 80.
- 'The really scientific…the function of religion.'
  From *Collected Works Vol. XII*, p. 322.
- 'A religious mind…not a religious mind.'
  From *Collected Works Vol. XII*, p. 270.

The Scientific Mind and the Religious Mind (with School Students)
- 'I want to…which society has set.'
  From *Krishnamurti on Education*, pp. 16-17.

Creative Energy
- 'Has one got…which is without motive?'
  From *Beginnings of Learning*, pp. 81-82.
- 'There is physical energy…emotional circus into it.'
  From *Beginnings of Learning*, pp. 92-93.

The Conscious and the Unconscious Mind
- 'Culture can only…to produce a result.'
  From *Collected Works Vol. IX*, pp.55-58.
- 'Do you work on…problems of your life.'
  From *Collected Works Vol. VIII*, pp. 13-15.

Common Consciousness
- 'The mind with its…ending nor beginning.'
  From *The Whole Movement of Life is Learning*, pp. 85-86.

The Significance of Subjects
- 'What is the significance…quality of integrity?'
  From Ojai 1980: Q&A 1, 6th May.

- 'Might we return...complexity of it?'
  From *A Wholly Different Way of Living*, pp. 62-63.

Right Action

- 'We are asking...bring about order.'
  From Madras 1977: Talk 3, 31st December.
- 'I wonder if you...only action.'
  From *Talks and Dialogues Saanen 1968*.

Excellence

- 'Is it necessary...what does education mean?'
  From Madras 1980-81: Talk 4, 4th January.
- 'Most people are...needs rest and care.'
  From *The Whole Movement of Life is Learning*, pp. 32-33
- 'We are dealing...these are not compassion.'
  From *The Wholeness of Life, p. 167*.

Education and Revolution

- 'Is it not important...bring about lasting peace.'
  From *Collected Works Vol. VIII*, pp. 141-42.

Love and Compassion

- 'Thought is memory...and final as death.'
  From *Krishnamurti's Journal*, p. 78.
- 'It is a great thing...then is there intelligence.'
  From *The Network of Thought, pp. 97- 98*.

Love, Compassion and Wisdom

- 'Is love pleasure?...yourself flowers wisdom.'
  From *Krishnamurti in India 1974-1975*, pp. 19-20.

Silence and Meditation
- 'Having laid the foundation...more and more.'
  From *Talks in Europe 1968*, pp. 41-43.
- 'Meditation is unpremeditated...go beyond them.'
  From Madras 1981: Talk 6, 11th January.

Meditation (with School Students)
- 'Do you know anything...I feel for you.'
  From *Beginnings of Learning*, pp. 79-80.

Meditation and Education
- 'Can we go into...the enormity of this.'
  From *Krishnamurti on Education*, pp. 171-77.

Made in the USA
San Bernardino, CA
27 April 2017